C-3416   CAREER EXAMINATION SERIES

This is your
PASSBOOK for...

Public Records Officer

Test Preparation Study Guide
Questions & Answers

COPYRIGHT NOTICE

This book is SOLELY intended for, is sold ONLY to, and its use is RESTRICTED to individual, bona fide applicants or candidates who qualify by virtue of having seriously filed applications for appropriate license, certificate, professional and/or promotional advancement, higher school matriculation, scholarship, or other legitimate requirements of education and/or governmental authorities.

This book is NOT intended for use, class instruction, tutoring, training, duplication, copying, reprinting, excerption, or adaptation, etc., by:

1) Other publishers
2) Proprietors and/or Instructors of "Coaching" and/or Preparatory Courses
3) Personnel and/or Training Divisions of commercial, industrial, and governmental organizations
4) Schools, colleges, or universities and/or their departments and staffs, including teachers and other personnel
5) Testing Agencies or Bureaus
6) Study groups which seek by the purchase of a single volume to copy and/or duplicate and/or adapt this material for use by the group as a whole without having purchased individual volumes for each of the members of the group
7) Et al.

Such persons would be in violation of appropriate Federal and State statutes.

PROVISION OF LICENSING AGREEMENTS – Recognized educational, commercial, industrial, and governmental institutions and organizations, and others legitimately engaged in educational pursuits, including training, testing, and measurement activities, may address request for a licensing agreement to the copyright owners, who will determine whether, and under what conditions, including fees and charges, the materials in this book may be used them. In other words, a licensing facility exists for the legitimate use of the material in this book on other than an individual basis. However, it is asseverated and affirmed here that the material in this book CANNOT be used without the receipt of the express permission of such a licensing agreement from the Publishers. Inquiries re licensing should be addressed to the company, attention rights and permissions department.

All rights reserved, including the right of reproduction in whole or in part, in any form or by any means, electronic or mechanical, including photocopying, recording, or by any information storage and retrieval system, without permission in writing from the Publisher.

Copyright © 2025 by
National Learning Corporation

212 Michael Drive, Syosset, NY 11791
(516) 921-8888 • www.passbooks.com
E-mail: info@passbooks.com

PASSBOOK® SERIES

THE *PASSBOOK® SERIES* has been created to prepare applicants and candidates for the ultimate academic battlefield – the examination room.

At some time in our lives, each and every one of us may be required to take an examination – for validation, matriculation, admission, qualification, registration, certification, or licensure.

Based on the assumption that every applicant or candidate has met the basic formal educational standards, has taken the required number of courses, and read the necessary texts, the *PASSBOOK® SERIES* furnishes the one special preparation which may assure passing with confidence, instead of failing with insecurity. Examination questions – together with answers – are furnished as the basic vehicle for study so that the mysteries of the examination and its compounding difficulties may be eliminated or diminished by a sure method.

This book is meant to help you pass your examination provided that you qualify and are serious in your objective.

The entire field is reviewed through the huge store of content information which is succinctly presented through a provocative and challenging approach – the question-and-answer method.

A climate of success is established by furnishing the correct answers at the end of each test.

You soon learn to recognize types of questions, forms of questions, and patterns of questioning. You may even begin to anticipate expected outcomes.

You perceive that many questions are repeated or adapted so that you can gain acute insights, which may enable you to score many sure points.

You learn how to confront new questions, or types of questions, and to attack them confidently and work out the correct answers.

You note objectives and emphases, and recognize pitfalls and dangers, so that you may make positive educational adjustments.

Moreover, you are kept fully informed in relation to new concepts, methods, practices, and directions in the field.

You discover that you are actually taking the examination all the time: you are preparing for the examination by "taking" an examination, not by reading extraneous and/or supererogatory textbooks.

In short, this PASSBOOK®, used directedly, should be an important factor in helping you to pass your test.

PUBLIC RECORDS OFFICER

DUTIES:
Under supervision, performs professional work and/or responsible supervisory work in archival, library or records management; performs related work.

SUBJECT OF EXAMINATION:
The written test may include questions on retrieval and retention of library, archives, or records materials; organization of materials; gathering of information; preparation of reports; supervisory and administrative duties; provision of assistance to facility users; repairing and conservation of materials; and other related areas.

HOW TO TAKE A TEST

I. YOU MUST PASS AN EXAMINATION

A. *WHAT EVERY CANDIDATE SHOULD KNOW*

Examination applicants often ask us for help in preparing for the written test. What can I study in advance? What kinds of questions will be asked? How will the test be given? How will the papers be graded?

As an applicant for a civil service examination, you may be wondering about some of these things. Our purpose here is to suggest effective methods of advance study and to describe civil service examinations.

Your chances for success on this examination can be increased if you know how to prepare. Those "pre-examination jitters" can be reduced if you know what to expect. You can even experience an adventure in good citizenship if you know why civil service exams are given.

B. *WHY ARE CIVIL SERVICE EXAMINATIONS GIVEN?*

Civil service examinations are important to you in two ways. As a citizen, you want public jobs filled by employees who know how to do their work. As a job seeker, you want a fair chance to compete for that job on an equal footing with other candidates. The best-known means of accomplishing this two-fold goal is the competitive examination.

Exams are widely publicized throughout the nation. They may be administered for jobs in federal, state, city, municipal, town or village governments or agencies.

Any citizen may apply, with some limitations, such as the age or residence of applicants. Your experience and education may be reviewed to see whether you meet the requirements for the particular examination. When these requirements exist, they are reasonable and applied consistently to all applicants. Thus, a competitive examination may cause you some uneasiness now, but it is your privilege and safeguard.

C. *HOW ARE CIVIL SERVICE EXAMS DEVELOPED?*

Examinations are carefully written by trained technicians who are specialists in the field known as "psychological measurement," in consultation with recognized authorities in the field of work that the test will cover. These experts recommend the subject matter areas or skills to be tested; only those knowledges or skills important to your success on the job are included. The most reliable books and source materials available are used as references. Together, the experts and technicians judge the difficulty level of the questions.

Test technicians know how to phrase questions so that the problem is clearly stated. Their ethics do not permit "trick" or "catch" questions. Questions may have been tried out on sample groups, or subjected to statistical analysis, to determine their usefulness.

Written tests are often used in combination with performance tests, ratings of training and experience, and oral interviews. All of these measures combine to form the best-known means of finding the right person for the right job.

II. HOW TO PASS THE WRITTEN TEST

A. NATURE OF THE EXAMINATION

To prepare intelligently for civil service examinations, you should know how they differ from school examinations you have taken. In school you were assigned certain definite pages to read or subjects to cover. The examination questions were quite detailed and usually emphasized memory. Civil service exams, on the other hand, try to discover your present ability to perform the duties of a position, plus your potentiality to learn these duties. In other words, a civil service exam attempts to predict how successful you will be. Questions cover such a broad area that they cannot be as minute and detailed as school exam questions.

In the public service similar kinds of work, or positions, are grouped together in one "class." This process is known as *position-classification*. All the positions in a class are paid according to the salary range for that class. One class title covers all of these positions, and they are all tested by the same examination.

B. FOUR BASIC STEPS

1) Study the announcement

How, then, can you know what subjects to study? Our best answer is: "Learn as much as possible about the class of positions for which you've applied." The exam will test the knowledge, skills and abilities needed to do the work.

Your most valuable source of information about the position you want is the official exam announcement. This announcement lists the training and experience qualifications. Check these standards and apply only if you come reasonably close to meeting them.

The brief description of the position in the examination announcement offers some clues to the subjects which will be tested. Think about the job itself. Review the duties in your mind. Can you perform them, or are there some in which you are rusty? Fill in the blank spots in your preparation.

Many jurisdictions preview the written test in the exam announcement by including a section called "Knowledge and Abilities Required," "Scope of the Examination," or some similar heading. Here you will find out specifically what fields will be tested.

2) Review your own background

Once you learn in general what the position is all about, and what you need to know to do the work, ask yourself which subjects you already know fairly well and which need improvement. You may wonder whether to concentrate on improving your strong areas or on building some background in your fields of weakness. When the announcement has specified "some knowledge" or "considerable knowledge," or has used adjectives like "beginning principles of…" or "advanced … methods," you can get a clue as to the number and difficulty of questions to be asked in any given field. More questions, and hence broader coverage, would be included for those subjects which are more important in the work. Now weigh your strengths and weaknesses against the job requirements and prepare accordingly.

3) Determine the level of the position

Another way to tell how intensively you should prepare is to understand the level of the job for which you are applying. Is it the entering level? In other words, is this the position in which beginners in a field of work are hired? Or is it an intermediate or advanced level? Sometimes this is indicated by such words as "Junior" or "Senior" in the class title. Other jurisdictions use Roman numerals to designate the level – Clerk I, Clerk II, for example. The word "Supervisor" sometimes appears in the title. If the level is not indicated by the title, check the description of duties. Will you be working under very close supervision, or will you have responsibility for independent decisions in this work?

4) Choose appropriate study materials

Now that you know the subjects to be examined and the relative amount of each subject to be covered, you can choose suitable study materials. For beginning level jobs, or even advanced ones, if you have a pronounced weakness in some aspect of your training, read a modern, standard textbook in that field. Be sure it is up to date and has general coverage. Such books are normally available at your library, and the librarian will be glad to help you locate one. For entry-level positions, questions of appropriate difficulty are chosen – neither highly advanced questions, nor those too simple. Such questions require careful thought but not advanced training.

If the position for which you are applying is technical or advanced, you will read more advanced, specialized material. If you are already familiar with the basic principles of your field, elementary textbooks would waste your time. Concentrate on advanced textbooks and technical periodicals. Think through the concepts and review difficult problems in your field.

These are all general sources. You can get more ideas on your own initiative, following these leads. For example, training manuals and publications of the government agency which employs workers in your field can be useful, particularly for technical and professional positions. A letter or visit to the government department involved may result in more specific study suggestions, and certainly will provide you with a more definite idea of the exact nature of the position you are seeking.

III. KINDS OF TESTS

Tests are used for purposes other than measuring knowledge and ability to perform specified duties. For some positions, it is equally important to test ability to make adjustments to new situations or to profit from training. In others, basic mental abilities not dependent on information are essential. Questions which test these things may not appear as pertinent to the duties of the position as those which test for knowledge and information. Yet they are often highly important parts of a fair examination. For very general questions, it is almost impossible to help you direct your study efforts. What we can do is to point out some of the more common of these general abilities needed in public service positions and describe some typical questions.

1) General information

Broad, general information has been found useful for predicting job success in some kinds of work. This is tested in a variety of ways, from vocabulary lists to questions about current events. Basic background in some field of work, such as sociology or economics, may be sampled in a group of questions. Often these are principles which have become familiar to most persons through exposure rather than through formal training. It is difficult to advise you how to study for these questions; being alert to the world around you is our best suggestion.

2) Verbal ability

An example of an ability needed in many positions is verbal or language ability. Verbal ability is, in brief, the ability to use and understand words. Vocabulary and grammar tests are typical measures of this ability. Reading comprehension or paragraph interpretation questions are common in many kinds of civil service tests. You are given a paragraph of written material and asked to find its central meaning.

3) Numerical ability

Number skills can be tested by the familiar arithmetic problem, by checking paired lists of numbers to see which are alike and which are different, or by interpreting charts and graphs. In the latter test, a graph may be printed in the test booklet which you are asked to use as the basis for answering questions.

4) Observation

A popular test for law-enforcement positions is the observation test. A picture is shown to you for several minutes, then taken away. Questions about the picture test your ability to observe both details and larger elements.

5) Following directions

In many positions in the public service, the employee must be able to carry out written instructions dependably and accurately. You may be given a chart with several columns, each column listing a variety of information. The questions require you to carry out directions involving the information given in the chart.

6) Skills and aptitudes

Performance tests effectively measure some manual skills and aptitudes. When the skill is one in which you are trained, such as typing or shorthand, you can practice. These tests are often very much like those given in business school or high school courses. For many of the other skills and aptitudes, however, no short-time preparation can be made. Skills and abilities natural to you or that you have developed throughout your lifetime are being tested.

Many of the general questions just described provide all the data needed to answer the questions and ask you to use your reasoning ability to find the answers. Your best preparation for these tests, as well as for tests of facts and ideas, is to be at your physical and mental best. You, no doubt, have your own methods of getting into an exam-taking mood and keeping "in shape." The next section lists some ideas on this subject.

IV. KINDS OF QUESTIONS

Only rarely is the "essay" question, which you answer in narrative form, used in civil service tests. Civil service tests are usually of the short-answer type. Full instructions for answering these questions will be given to you at the examination. But in case this is your first experience with short-answer questions and separate answer sheets, here is what you need to know:

1) Multiple-choice Questions

Most popular of the short-answer questions is the "multiple choice" or "best answer" question. It can be used, for example, to test for factual knowledge, ability to solve problems or judgment in meeting situations found at work.

A multiple-choice question is normally one of three types—
- It can begin with an incomplete statement followed by several possible endings. You are to find the one ending which *best* completes the statement, although some of the others may not be entirely wrong.
- It can also be a complete statement in the form of a question which is answered by choosing one of the statements listed.

- It can be in the form of a problem – again you select the best answer.

Here is an example of a multiple-choice question with a discussion which should give you some clues as to the method for choosing the right answer:

When an employee has a complaint about his assignment, the action which will *best* help him overcome his difficulty is to
- A. discuss his difficulty with his coworkers
- B. take the problem to the head of the organization
- C. take the problem to the person who gave him the assignment
- D. say nothing to anyone about his complaint

In answering this question, you should study each of the choices to find which is best. Consider choice "A" – Certainly an employee may discuss his complaint with fellow employees, but no change or improvement can result, and the complaint remains unresolved. Choice "B" is a poor choice since the head of the organization probably does not know what assignment you have been given, and taking your problem to him is known as "going over the head" of the supervisor. The supervisor, or person who made the assignment, is the person who can clarify it or correct any injustice. Choice "C" is, therefore, correct. To say nothing, as in choice "D," is unwise. Supervisors have and interest in knowing the problems employees are facing, and the employee is seeking a solution to his problem.

2) True/False Questions

The "true/false" or "right/wrong" form of question is sometimes used. Here a complete statement is given. Your job is to decide whether the statement is right or wrong.

SAMPLE: A roaming cell-phone call to a nearby city costs less than a non-roaming call to a distant city.

This statement is wrong, or false, since roaming calls are more expensive.

This is not a complete list of all possible question forms, although most of the others are variations of these common types. You will always get complete directions for answering questions. Be sure you understand *how* to mark your answers – ask questions until you do.

V. RECORDING YOUR ANSWERS

Computer terminals are used more and more today for many different kinds of exams.

For an examination with very few applicants, you may be told to record your answers in the test booklet itself. Separate answer sheets are much more common. If this separate answer sheet is to be scored by machine – and this is often the case – it is highly important that you mark your answers correctly in order to get credit.

An electronic scoring machine is often used in civil service offices because of the speed with which papers can be scored. Machine-scored answer sheets must be marked with a pencil, which will be given to you. This pencil has a high graphite content which responds to the electronic scoring machine. As a matter of fact, stray dots may register as answers, so do not let your pencil rest on the answer sheet while you are pondering the correct answer. Also, if your pencil lead breaks or is otherwise defective, ask for another.

Since the answer sheet will be dropped in a slot in the scoring machine, be careful not to bend the corners or get the paper crumpled.

The answer sheet normally has five vertical columns of numbers, with 30 numbers to a column. These numbers correspond to the question numbers in your test booklet. After each number, going across the page are four or five pairs of dotted lines. These short dotted lines have small letters or numbers above them. The first two pairs may also have a "T" or "F" above the letters. This indicates that the first two pairs only are to be used if the questions are of the true-false type. If the questions are multiple choice, disregard the "T" and "F" and pay attention only to the small letters or numbers.

Answer your questions in the manner of the sample that follows:

32. The largest city in the United States is
    A. Washington, D.C.
    B. New York City
    C. Chicago
    D. Detroit
    E. San Francisco

1) Choose the answer you think is best. (New York City is the largest, so "B" is correct.)
2) Find the row of dotted lines numbered the same as the question you are answering. (Find row number 32)
3) Find the pair of dotted lines corresponding to the answer. (Find the pair of lines under the mark "B.")
4) Make a solid black mark between the dotted lines.

VI. BEFORE THE TEST

Common sense will help you find procedures to follow to get ready for an examination. Too many of us, however, overlook these sensible measures. Indeed, nervousness and fatigue have been found to be the most serious reasons why applicants fail to do their best on civil service tests. Here is a list of reminders:

- Begin your preparation early – Don't wait until the last minute to go scurrying around for books and materials or to find out what the position is all about.
- Prepare continuously – An hour a night for a week is better than an all-night cram session. This has been definitely established. What is more, a night a week for a month will return better dividends than crowding your study into a shorter period of time.
- Locate the place of the exam – You have been sent a notice telling you when and where to report for the examination. If the location is in a different town or otherwise unfamiliar to you, it would be well to inquire the best route and learn something about the building.
- Relax the night before the test – Allow your mind to rest. Do not study at all that night. Plan some mild recreation or diversion; then go to bed early and get a good night's sleep.
- Get up early enough to make a leisurely trip to the place for the test – This way unforeseen events, traffic snarls, unfamiliar buildings, etc. will not upset you.
- Dress comfortably – A written test is not a fashion show. You will be known by number and not by name, so wear something comfortable.

- Leave excess paraphernalia at home – Shopping bags and odd bundles will get in your way. You need bring only the items mentioned in the official notice you received; usually everything you need is provided. Do not bring reference books to the exam. They will only confuse those last minutes and be taken away from you when in the test room.
- Arrive somewhat ahead of time – If because of transportation schedules you must get there very early, bring a newspaper or magazine to take your mind off yourself while waiting.
- Locate the examination room – When you have found the proper room, you will be directed to the seat or part of the room where you will sit. Sometimes you are given a sheet of instructions to read while you are waiting. Do not fill out any forms until you are told to do so; just read them and be prepared.
- Relax and prepare to listen to the instructions
- If you have any physical problem that may keep you from doing your best, be sure to tell the test administrator. If you are sick or in poor health, you really cannot do your best on the exam. You can come back and take the test some other time.

VII. AT THE TEST

The day of the test is here and you have the test booklet in your hand. The temptation to get going is very strong. Caution! There is more to success than knowing the right answers. You must know how to identify your papers and understand variations in the type of short-answer question used in this particular examination. Follow these suggestions for maximum results from your efforts:

1) Cooperate with the monitor

The test administrator has a duty to create a situation in which you can be as much at ease as possible. He will give instructions, tell you when to begin, check to see that you are marking your answer sheet correctly, and so on. He is not there to guard you, although he will see that your competitors do not take unfair advantage. He wants to help you do your best.

2) Listen to all instructions

Don't jump the gun! Wait until you understand all directions. In most civil service tests you get more time than you need to answer the questions. So don't be in a hurry. Read each word of instructions until you clearly understand the meaning. Study the examples, listen to all announcements and follow directions. Ask questions if you do not understand what to do.

3) Identify your papers

Civil service exams are usually identified by number only. You will be assigned a number; you must not put your name on your test papers. Be sure to copy your number correctly. Since more than one exam may be given, copy your exact examination title.

4) Plan your time

Unless you are told that a test is a "speed" or "rate of work" test, speed itself is usually not important. Time enough to answer all the questions will be provided, but this does not mean that you have all day. An overall time limit has been set. Divide the total time (in minutes) by the number of questions to determine the approximate time you have for each question.

5) Do not linger over difficult questions

If you come across a difficult question, mark it with a paper clip (useful to have along) and come back to it when you have been through the booklet. One caution if you do this – be sure to skip a number on your answer sheet as well. Check often to be sure that you have not lost your place and that you are marking in the row numbered the same as the question you are answering.

6) Read the questions

Be sure you know what the question asks! Many capable people are unsuccessful because they failed to *read* the questions correctly.

7) Answer all questions

Unless you have been instructed that a penalty will be deducted for incorrect answers, it is better to guess than to omit a question.

8) Speed tests

It is often better NOT to guess on speed tests. It has been found that on timed tests people are tempted to spend the last few seconds before time is called in marking answers at random – without even reading them – in the hope of picking up a few extra points. To discourage this practice, the instructions may warn you that your score will be "corrected" for guessing. That is, a penalty will be applied. The incorrect answers will be deducted from the correct ones, or some other penalty formula will be used.

9) Review your answers

If you finish before time is called, go back to the questions you guessed or omitted to give them further thought. Review other answers if you have time.

10) Return your test materials

If you are ready to leave before others have finished or time is called, take ALL your materials to the monitor and leave quietly. Never take any test material with you. The monitor can discover whose papers are not complete, and taking a test booklet may be grounds for disqualification.

VIII. EXAMINATION TECHNIQUES

1) Read the general instructions carefully. These are usually printed on the first page of the exam booklet. As a rule, these instructions refer to the timing of the examination; the fact that you should not start work until the signal and must stop work at a signal, etc. If there are any *special* instructions, such as a choice of questions to be answered, make sure that you note this instruction carefully.

2) When you are ready to start work on the examination, that is as soon as the signal has been given, read the instructions to each question booklet, underline any key words or phrases, such as *least, best, outline, describe* and the like. In this way you will tend to answer as requested rather than discover on reviewing your paper that you *listed without describing*, that you selected the *worst* choice rather than the *best* choice, etc.

3) If the examination is of the objective or multiple-choice type – that is, each question will also give a series of possible answers: A, B, C or D, and you are called upon to select the best answer and write the letter next to that answer on your answer paper – it is advisable to start answering each question in turn. There may be anywhere from 50 to 100 such questions in the three or four hours allotted and you can see how much time would be taken if you read through all the questions before beginning to answer any. Furthermore, if you come across a question or group of questions which you know would be difficult to answer, it would undoubtedly affect your handling of all the other questions.

4) If the examination is of the essay type and contains but a few questions, it is a moot point as to whether you should read all the questions before starting to answer any one. Of course, if you are given a choice – say five out of seven and the like – then it is essential to read all the questions so you can eliminate the two that are most difficult. If, however, you are asked to answer all the questions, there may be danger in trying to answer the easiest one first because you may find that you will spend too much time on it. The best technique is to answer the first question, then proceed to the second, etc.

5) Time your answers. Before the exam begins, write down the time it started, then add the time allowed for the examination and write down the time it must be completed, then divide the time available somewhat as follows:
   - If 3-1/2 hours are allowed, that would be 210 minutes. If you have 80 objective-type questions, that would be an average of 2-1/2 minutes per question. Allow yourself no more than 2 minutes per question, or a total of 160 minutes, which will permit about 50 minutes to review.
   - If for the time allotment of 210 minutes there are 7 essay questions to answer, that would average about 30 minutes a question. Give yourself only 25 minutes per question so that you have about 35 minutes to review.

6) The most important instruction is to *read each question* and make sure you know what is wanted. The second most important instruction is to *time yourself properly* so that you answer every question. The third most important instruction is to *answer every question*. Guess if you have to but include something for each question. Remember that you will receive no credit for a blank and will probably receive some credit if you write something in answer to an essay question. If you guess a letter – say "B" for a multiple-choice question – you may have guessed right. If you leave a blank as an answer to a multiple-choice question, the examiners may respect your feelings but it will not add a point to your score. Some exams may penalize you for wrong answers, so in such cases *only*, you may not want to guess unless you have some basis for your answer.

7) Suggestions
   a. Objective-type questions
      1. Examine the question booklet for proper sequence of pages and questions
      2. Read all instructions carefully
      3. Skip any question which seems too difficult; return to it after all other questions have been answered
      4. Apportion your time properly; do not spend too much time on any single question or group of questions

5. Note and underline key words – *all, most, fewest, least, best, worst, same, opposite,* etc.
6. Pay particular attention to negatives
7. Note unusual option, e.g., unduly long, short, complex, different or similar in content to the body of the question
8. Observe the use of "hedging" words – *probably, may, most likely,* etc.
9. Make sure that your answer is put next to the same number as the question
10. Do not second-guess unless you have good reason to believe the second answer is definitely more correct
11. Cross out original answer if you decide another answer is more accurate; do not erase until you are ready to hand your paper in
12. Answer all questions; guess unless instructed otherwise
13. Leave time for review

   b. Essay questions
   1. Read each question carefully
   2. Determine exactly what is wanted. Underline key words or phrases.
   3. Decide on outline or paragraph answer
   4. Include many different points and elements unless asked to develop any one or two points or elements
   5. Show impartiality by giving pros and cons unless directed to select one side only
   6. Make and write down any assumptions you find necessary to answer the questions
   7. Watch your English, grammar, punctuation and choice of words
   8. Time your answers; don't crowd material

8) Answering the essay question

Most essay questions can be answered by framing the specific response around several key words or ideas. Here are a few such key words or ideas:

M's: manpower, materials, methods, money, management
P's: purpose, program, policy, plan, procedure, practice, problems, pitfalls, personnel, public relations

   a. Six basic steps in handling problems:
   1. Preliminary plan and background development
   2. Collect information, data and facts
   3. Analyze and interpret information, data and facts
   4. Analyze and develop solutions as well as make recommendations
   5. Prepare report and sell recommendations
   6. Install recommendations and follow up effectiveness

   b. Pitfalls to avoid
   1. *Taking things for granted* – A statement of the situation does not necessarily imply that each of the elements is necessarily true; for example, a complaint may be invalid and biased so that all that can be taken for granted is that a complaint has been registered

2. *Considering only one side of a situation* – Wherever possible, indicate several alternatives and then point out the reasons you selected the best one
3. *Failing to indicate follow up* – Whenever your answer indicates action on your part, make certain that you will take proper follow-up action to see how successful your recommendations, procedures or actions turn out to be
4. *Taking too long in answering any single question* – Remember to time your answers properly

IX. AFTER THE TEST

Scoring procedures differ in detail among civil service jurisdictions although the general principles are the same. Whether the papers are hand-scored or graded by machine we have described, they are nearly always graded by number. That is, the person who marks the paper knows only the number – never the name – of the applicant. Not until all the papers have been graded will they be matched with names. If other tests, such as training and experience or oral interview ratings have been given, scores will be combined. Different parts of the examination usually have different weights. For example, the written test might count 60 percent of the final grade, and a rating of training and experience 40 percent. In many jurisdictions, veterans will have a certain number of points added to their grades.

After the final grade has been determined, the names are placed in grade order and an eligible list is established. There are various methods for resolving ties between those who get the same final grade – probably the most common is to place first the name of the person whose application was received first. Job offers are made from the eligible list in the order the names appear on it. You will be notified of your grade and your rank as soon as all these computations have been made. This will be done as rapidly as possible.

People who are found to meet the requirements in the announcement are called "eligibles." Their names are put on a list of eligible candidates. An eligible's chances of getting a job depend on how high he stands on this list and how fast agencies are filling jobs from the list.

When a job is to be filled from a list of eligibles, the agency asks for the names of people on the list of eligibles for that job. When the civil service commission receives this request, it sends to the agency the names of the three people highest on this list. Or, if the job to be filled has specialized requirements, the office sends the agency the names of the top three persons who meet these requirements from the general list.

The appointing officer makes a choice from among the three people whose names were sent to him. If the selected person accepts the appointment, the names of the others are put back on the list to be considered for future openings.

That is the rule in hiring from all kinds of eligible lists, whether they are for typist, carpenter, chemist, or something else. For every vacancy, the appointing officer has his choice of any one of the top three eligibles on the list. This explains why the person whose name is on top of the list sometimes does not get an appointment when some of the persons lower on the list do. If the appointing officer chooses the second or third eligible, the No. 1 eligible does not get a job at once, but stays on the list until he is appointed or the list is terminated.

X. HOW TO PASS THE INTERVIEW TEST

The examination for which you applied requires an oral interview test. You have already taken the written test and you are now being called for the interview test – the final part of the formal examination.

You may think that it is not possible to prepare for an interview test and that there are no procedures to follow during an interview. Our purpose is to point out some things you can do in advance that will help you and some good rules to follow and pitfalls to avoid while you are being interviewed.

What is an interview supposed to test?

The written examination is designed to test the technical knowledge and competence of the candidate; the oral is designed to evaluate intangible qualities, not readily measured otherwise, and to establish a list showing the relative fitness of each candidate – as measured against his competitors – for the position sought. Scoring is not on the basis of "right" and "wrong," but on a sliding scale of values ranging from "not passable" to "outstanding." As a matter of fact, it is possible to achieve a relatively low score without a single "incorrect" answer because of evident weakness in the qualities being measured.

Occasionally, an examination may consist entirely of an oral test – either an individual or a group oral. In such cases, information is sought concerning the technical knowledges and abilities of the candidate, since there has been no written examination for this purpose. More commonly, however, an oral test is used to supplement a written examination.

Who conducts interviews?

The composition of oral boards varies among different jurisdictions. In nearly all, a representative of the personnel department serves as chairman. One of the members of the board may be a representative of the department in which the candidate would work. In some cases, "outside experts" are used, and, frequently, a businessman or some other representative of the general public is asked to serve. Labor and management or other special groups may be represented. The aim is to secure the services of experts in the appropriate field.

However the board is composed, it is a good idea (and not at all improper or unethical) to ascertain in advance of the interview who the members are and what groups they represent. When you are introduced to them, you will have some idea of their backgrounds and interests, and at least you will not stutter and stammer over their names.

What should be done before the interview?

While knowledge about the board members is useful and takes some of the surprise element out of the interview, there is other preparation which is more substantive. It *is* possible to prepare for an oral interview – in several ways:

1) Keep a copy of your application and review it carefully before the interview

This may be the only document before the oral board, and the starting point of the interview. Know what education and experience you have listed there, and the sequence and dates of all of it. Sometimes the board will ask you to review the highlights of your experience for them; you should not have to hem and haw doing it.

2) Study the class specification and the examination announcement

Usually, the oral board has one or both of these to guide them. The qualities, characteristics or knowledges required by the position sought are stated in these documents. They offer valuable clues as to the nature of the oral interview. For example, if the job involves supervisory responsibilities, the announcement will usually indicate that knowledge of modern supervisory methods and the qualifications of the candidate as a supervisor will be tested. If so, you can expect such questions, frequently in the form of a hypothetical situation which you are expected to solve. NEVER go into an oral without knowledge of the duties and responsibilities of the job you seek.

3) Think through each qualification required

Try to visualize the kind of questions you would ask if you were a board member. How well could you answer them? Try especially to appraise your own knowledge and background in each area, *measured against the job sought*, and identify any areas in which you are weak. Be critical and realistic – do not flatter yourself.

4) Do some general reading in areas in which you feel you may be weak

For example, if the job involves supervision and your past experience has NOT, some general reading in supervisory methods and practices, particularly in the field of human relations, might be useful. Do NOT study agency procedures or detailed manuals. The oral board will be testing your understanding and capacity, not your memory.

5) Get a good night's sleep and watch your general health and mental attitude

You will want a clear head at the interview. Take care of a cold or any other minor ailment, and of course, no hangovers.

What should be done on the day of the interview?

Now comes the day of the interview itself. Give yourself plenty of time to get there. Plan to arrive somewhat ahead of the scheduled time, particularly if your appointment is in the fore part of the day. If a previous candidate fails to appear, the board might be ready for you a bit early. By early afternoon an oral board is almost invariably behind schedule if there are many candidates, and you may have to wait. Take along a book or magazine to read, or your application to review, but leave any extraneous material in the waiting room when you go in for your interview. In any event, relax and compose yourself.

The matter of dress is important. The board is forming impressions about you – from your experience, your manners, your attitude, and your appearance. Give your personal appearance careful attention. Dress your best, but not your flashiest. Choose conservative, appropriate clothing, and be sure it is immaculate. This is a business interview, and your appearance should indicate that you regard it as such. Besides, being well groomed and properly dressed will help boost your confidence.

Sooner or later, someone will call your name and escort you into the interview room. *This is it.* From here on you are on your own. It is too late for any more preparation. But remember, you asked for this opportunity to prove your fitness, and you are here because your request was granted.

What happens when you go in?

The usual sequence of events will be as follows: The clerk (who is often the board stenographer) will introduce you to the chairman of the oral board, who will introduce you to the other members of the board. Acknowledge the introductions before you sit down. Do not be surprised if you find a microphone facing you or a stenotypist sitting by. Oral interviews are usually recorded in the event of an appeal or other review.

Usually the chairman of the board will open the interview by reviewing the highlights of your education and work experience from your application – primarily for the benefit of the other members of the board, as well as to get the material into the record. Do not interrupt or comment unless there is an error or significant misinterpretation; if that is the case, do not hesitate. But do not quibble about insignificant matters. Also, he will usually ask you some question about your education, experience or your present job – partly to get you to start talking and to establish the interviewing "rapport." He may start the actual questioning, or turn it over to one of the other members. Frequently, each member undertakes the questioning on a particular area, one in which he is perhaps most competent, so you can expect each member to participate in the examination. Because time is limited, you may also expect some rather abrupt switches in the direction the questioning takes, so do not be upset by it. Normally, a board member will not pursue a single line of questioning unless he discovers a particular strength or weakness.

After each member has participated, the chairman will usually ask whether any member has any further questions, then will ask you if you have anything you wish to add. Unless you are expecting this question, it may floor you. Worse, it may start you off on an extended, extemporaneous speech. The board is not usually seeking more information. The question is principally to offer you a last opportunity to present further qualifications or to indicate that you have nothing to add. So, if you feel that a significant qualification or characteristic has been overlooked, it is proper to point it out in a sentence or so. Do not compliment the board on the thoroughness of their examination – they have been sketchy, and you know it. If you wish, merely say, "No thank you, I have nothing further to add." This is a point where you can "talk yourself out" of a good impression or fail to present an important bit of information. Remember, *you close the interview yourself.*

The chairman will then say, "That is all, Mr. _____, thank you." Do not be startled; the interview is over, and quicker than you think. Thank him, gather your belongings and take your leave. Save your sigh of relief for the other side of the door.

How to put your best foot forward

Throughout this entire process, you may feel that the board individually and collectively is trying to pierce your defenses, seek out your hidden weaknesses and embarrass and confuse you. Actually, this is not true. They are obliged to make an appraisal of your qualifications for the job you are seeking, and they want to see you in your best light. Remember, they must interview all candidates and a non-cooperative candidate may become a failure in spite of their best efforts to bring out his qualifications. Here are 15 suggestions that will help you:

1) Be natural – Keep your attitude confident, not cocky

If you are not confident that you can do the job, do not expect the board to be. Do not apologize for your weaknesses, try to bring out your strong points. The board is interested in a positive, not negative, presentation. Cockiness will antagonize any board member and make him wonder if you are covering up a weakness by a false show of strength.

2) Get comfortable, but don't lounge or sprawl

Sit erectly but not stiffly. A careless posture may lead the board to conclude that you are careless in other things, or at least that you are not impressed by the importance of the occasion. Either conclusion is natural, even if incorrect. Do not fuss with your clothing, a pencil or an ashtray. Your hands may occasionally be useful to emphasize a point; do not let them become a point of distraction.

3) Do not wisecrack or make small talk

This is a serious situation, and your attitude should show that you consider it as such. Further, the time of the board is limited – they do not want to waste it, and neither should you.

4) Do not exaggerate your experience or abilities

In the first place, from information in the application or other interviews and sources, the board may know more about you than you think. Secondly, you probably will not get away with it. An experienced board is rather adept at spotting such a situation, so do not take the chance.

5) If you know a board member, do not make a point of it, yet do not hide it

Certainly you are not fooling him, and probably not the other members of the board. Do not try to take advantage of your acquaintanceship – it will probably do you little good.

6) Do not dominate the interview

Let the board do that. They will give you the clues – do not assume that you have to do all the talking. Realize that the board has a number of questions to ask you, and do not try to take up all the interview time by showing off your extensive knowledge of the answer to the first one.

7) Be attentive

You only have 20 minutes or so, and you should keep your attention at its sharpest throughout. When a member is addressing a problem or question to you, give him your undivided attention. Address your reply principally to him, but do not exclude the other board members.

8) Do not interrupt

A board member may be stating a problem for you to analyze. He will ask you a question when the time comes. Let him state the problem, and wait for the question.

9) Make sure you understand the question

Do not try to answer until you are sure what the question is. If it is not clear, restate it in your own words or ask the board member to clarify it for you. However, do not haggle about minor elements.

10) Reply promptly but not hastily

A common entry on oral board rating sheets is "candidate responded readily," or "candidate hesitated in replies." Respond as promptly and quickly as you can, but do not jump to a hasty, ill-considered answer.

11) Do not be peremptory in your answers

A brief answer is proper – but do not fire your answer back. That is a losing game from your point of view. The board member can probably ask questions much faster than you can answer them.

12) Do not try to create the answer you think the board member wants

He is interested in what kind of mind you have and how it works – not in playing games. Furthermore, he can usually spot this practice and will actually grade you down on it.

13) Do not switch sides in your reply merely to agree with a board member

Frequently, a member will take a contrary position merely to draw you out and to see if you are willing and able to defend your point of view. Do not start a debate, yet do not surrender a good position. If a position is worth taking, it is worth defending.

14) Do not be afraid to admit an error in judgment if you are shown to be wrong
   The board knows that you are forced to reply without any opportunity for careful consideration. Your answer may be demonstrably wrong. If so, admit it and get on with the interview.

15) Do not dwell at length on your present job
   The opening question may relate to your present assignment. Answer the question but do not go into an extended discussion. You are being examined for a *new* job, not your present one. As a matter of fact, try to phrase ALL your answers in terms of the job for which you are being examined.

Basis of Rating
   Probably you will forget most of these "do's" and "don'ts" when you walk into the oral interview room. Even remembering them all will not ensure you a passing grade. Perhaps you did not have the qualifications in the first place. But remembering them will help you to put your best foot forward, without treading on the toes of the board members.
   Rumor and popular opinion to the contrary notwithstanding, an oral board wants you to make the best appearance possible. They know you are under pressure – but they also want to see how you respond to it as a guide to what your reaction would be under the pressures of the job you seek. They will be influenced by the degree of poise you display, the personal traits you show and the manner in which you respond.

ABOUT THIS BOOK

   This book contains tests divided into Examination Sections. Go through each test, answering every question in the margin. We have also attached a sample answer sheet at the back of the book that can be removed and used. At the end of each test look at the answer key and check your answers. On the ones you got wrong, look at the right answer choice and learn. Do not fill in the answers first. Do not memorize the questions and answers, but understand the answer and principles involved. On your test, the questions will likely be different from the samples. Questions are changed and new ones added. If you understand these past questions you should have success with any changes that arise. Tests may consist of several types of questions. We have additional books on each subject should more study be advisable or necessary for you. Finally, the more you study, the better prepared you will be. This book is intended to be the last thing you study before you walk into the examination room. Prior study of relevant texts is also recommended. NLC publishes some of these in our Fundamental Series. Knowledge and good sense are important factors in passing your exam. Good luck also helps. So now study this Passbook, absorb the material contained within and take that knowledge into the examination. Then do your best to pass that exam.

EXAMINATION SECTION

EXAMINATION SECTION
TEST 1

DIRECTIONS: Each question or incomplete statement is followed by several suggested answers or completions. Select the one that BEST answers the question or completes the statement. *PRINT THE LETTER OF THE CORRECT ANSWER IN THE SPACE AT THE RIGHT.*

1. Records of one type or another are kept in every office. The MOST important of the following reasons for the supervisor of a clerical or stenographic unit to keep statistical records of the work done in his unit is generally to

    A. supply basic information needed in planning the work of the unit
    B. obtain statistics for comparison with other units
    C. serve as the basis for unsatisfactory employee evaluation
    D. provide the basis for special research projects on program budgeting

    1.____

2. It is better for an employee to report and be responsible directly to several supervisors than to report and be responsible to only one supervisor.
   This statement directly CONTRADICTS the supervisory principle generally known as

    A. span of control
    B. unity of command
    C. delegation of authority
    D. accountability

    2.____

3. The one of the following which would MOST likely lead to friction among clerks in a unit is for the unit supervisor to

    A. defend the actions of his clerks when discussing them with his own supervisor
    B. praise each of his clerks "in confidence" as the best clerk in the unit
    C. get his men to work together as a team in completing the work of the unit
    D. consider the point of view of the rank and file clerks when assigning unpleasant tasks

    3.____

4. You become aware that one of the employees you supervise has failed to follow correct procedure and has been permitting various reports to be prepared, typed, and transmitted improperly.
   The BEST action for you to take FIRST in this situation is to

    A. order the employee to review all departmental procedures and reprimand him for having violated them
    B. warn the employee that he must obey regulations because uniformity is essential for effective departmental operation
    C. confer with the employee both about his failure to follow regulations and his reasons for doing so
    D. watch the employee's work very closely in the future but say nothing about this violation

    4.____

5. The supervisory clerk who would be MOST likely to have poor control over his subordinates is the one who

    A. goes to unusually great lengths to try to win their approval
    B. pitches in with the work they are doing during periods of heavy workload when no extra help can be obtained

    5.____

C. encourages and helps his subordinates toward advancement
D. considers suggestions from his subordinates before establishing new work procedures involving them

6. Suppose that a clerk who has been transferred to your office from another division in your agency because of difficulties with his supervisor has been placed under your supervision.
   The BEST course of action for you to take FIRST is to

   A. instruct the clerk in the duties he will be performing in your office and make him feel "wanted" in his new position
   B. analyze the clerk's past grievance to determine if the transfer was the best solution to the problem
   C. advise him of the difficulties that his former supervisor had with other employees and encourage him not to feel badly about the transfer
   D. warn him that you will not tolerate any nonsense and that he will be under continuous surveillance while assigned to you

7. A certain office supervisor takes the initiative to represent his employees' interests related to working conditions, opportunities for advancement, etc. to his own supervisor and the administrative levels of the agency. This supervisor's actions will MOST probably have the effect of

   A. preventing employees from developing individual initiative in their work goals
   B. encouraging employees to compete openly for the special attention of their supervisor
   C. depriving employees of the opportunity to be represented by persons and/or unions of their own choosing
   D. building employee confidence in their supervisor and a spirit of cooperation in their work

8. Suppose that you have been promoted, assigned as a supervisor of a certain unit and asked to reorganize its functions so that specific routine procedures can be established. Before deciding which routines to establish, the FIRST of the following steps you should take is to

   A. decide who will perform each task in the routine
   B. determine the purpose to be served by each routine procedure
   C. outline the sequence of steps in each routine to be established
   D. calculate if more staff will be needed to carry out the new procedures

9. When routine procedures covering the ordinary work of an office are established, the supervisor of the office tends to be relieved of the need to

   A. make repeated decisions on the handling of recurring similar situations
   B. check the accuracy of the work completed by his subordinates
   C. train his subordinates in new work procedures
   D. plan and schedule the work of his office

10. Of the following, the method which would be LEAST helpful to a supervisor in effectively applying the principles of on-the-job safety to the daily work of his unit is for him to

A. initiate corrections of unsafe layouts of equipment and unsafe work processes
B. take charge of operations that are not routine to make certain that safety precautions are established and observed
C. continue to "talk safety" and promote safety consciousness in his subordinates
D. figure the cost of all accidents which could possibly occur on the job

11. A clerk is assigned to serve as receptionist for a large and busy office. Although many members of the public visit this office, the clerk often experiences periods of time in which he has nothing to do.
In these circumstances, the MOST advisable of the following actions for the supervisor to take is to

    A. assign a number of relatively low priority clerical jobs to the receptionist to do in the slow periods
    B. regularly rotate this assignment so that all the clerks experience this lighter work load
    C. assign the receptionist job as part of the duties of a number of clerks whose desks are nearest the reception room
    D. overlook the situation, since most of the receptionist's time is spent in performing a necessary and meaningful function

12. For a supervisor to require all stenographers in a stenographic pool to produce the same amount of work on a particular day is

    A. *advisable;* since it will prove that the supervisor plays no favorites
    B. *fair;* since all the stenographers are receiving approximately the same salary, their output should be equivalent
    C. *not necessary;* since the fast workers will compensate for the slow workers
    D. *not realistic;* since individual differences in abilities and work assignment must be taken into consideration

13. The establishment of a centralized typing pool to service the various units in an organization is MOST likely to be worthwhile when there is

    A. wide fluctuation from time to time in the needs of the various units for typing service
    B. a large volume of typing work to be done in each of the units
    C. a need by each unit for different kinds of typing service
    D. a training program in operation to develop and maintain typing skills

14. A newly appointed supervisor should learn as much as possible about the backgrounds of his subordinates. This statement is generally CORRECT because

    A. knowing their backgrounds assures they will be treated objectively, equally, and without favor
    B. effective handling of subordinates is based upon knowledge of their individual differences
    C. subordinates perform more efficiently under one supervisor than under another
    D. subordinates have confidence in a supervisor who knows all about them

15. The use of electronic computers in modern businesses has produced many changes in office and information management. Of the following, it would NOT be correct to state that computer utilization

A. broadens the scope of managerial and supervisory authority
B. establishes uniformity in the processing and reporting of information
C. cuts costs by reducing the personnel needed for efficient office operation
D. supplies management rapidly with up-to-date data to facilitate decision-making

16. The CHIEF advantage of having a single, large open office instead of small partitioned ones for a clerical unit or stenographic pool is that the single, large open office

    A. affords privacy without isolation for all office workers not directly dealing with the public
    B. assures the smoother, more continuous inter-office flow of work that is essential for efficient work production
    C. facilitates the office supervisor's visual control over and communication with his subordinates
    D. permits a more decorative and functional arrangement of office furniture and machines

17. When a supervisor provides a new employee with the information necessary for a basic knowledge and a general understanding of practices and procedures of the agency, he is applying the type of training generally known as _____ training.

    A. pre-employment   B. induction
    C. on-the-job   D. supervisory

18. Many government agencies require the approval by a central forms control unit of the design and reproduction of new office forms.
    The one of the following results of this procedure that is a DISADVANTAGE is that requiring prior approval of a central forms control unit USUALLY

    A. limits the distribution of forms to those offices with justifiable reasons for receiving them
    B. permits checking whether existing forms or modifications of them are in line with current agency needs
    C. encourages reliance on only the central office to set up all additional forms when needed
    D. provides for someone with a specialized knowledge of forms design to review and criticize new and revised forms

19. Suppose that a large quantity of information is in the files which are located a good distance from your desk. Almost every worker in your office must use these files constantly. Your duties in particular require that you daily refer to about 25 of the same items. They are short, one-page items distributed throughout the files.
    In this situation, your BEST course would be to

    A. take the items that you use daily from the files and keep them on your desk, inserting "out cards" in their place
    B. go to the files each time you need the information so that the items will be there when other workers need them
    C. make xerox copies of the information you use most frequently and keep them in your desk for ready reference
    D. label the items you use most often with different colored tabs for immediate identification

20. Of the following, the MOST important advantage of preparing manuals of office procedures in loose-leaf form is that this form

    A. permits several employees to use different sections simultaneously
    B. facilitates the addition of new material and the removal of obsolete material
    C. is more readily arranged in alphabetical order
    D. reduces the need for cross-references to locate material carried under several headings

21. Suppose that you establish a new clerical procedure for the unit you supervise.
    Your keeping a close check on the time required by your staff to handle the new procedure is wise MAINLY because such a check will find out

    A. whether your subordinates know how to handle the new procedure
    B. whether a revision of the unit's work schedule will be necessary as a result of the new procedure
    C. what attitude your employees have toward the new procedure
    D. what alterations in job descriptions will be necessitated by the new procedure

22. From the viewpoint of an office supervisor, the BEST of the following reasons for distributing the incoming mail *before* the beginning of the regular work day is that

    A. distribution can be handled quickly and most efficiently at that time
    B. distribution later in the day may be distracting to or interfere with other employees
    C. the employees who distribute the mail can then perform other tasks during the rest of the day
    D. office activities for the day based on the mail may then be started promptly

23. Suppose you are the head of a unit with ten staff members who are located in several different rooms. If you want to inform your staff of a *minor* change in procedure, the BEST and LEAST expensive way of doing so would usually be to

    A. send a mimeographed copy to each staff member
    B. call a special staff meeting and announce the change
    C. circulate a memo, having each staff member initial it
    D. have a clerk tell each member of the staff about the change

24. The numbered statements below relate to the stenographic skill of taking dictation.
    According to authorities on secretarial practices, which of these are GENERALLY recommended guides to development of efficient stenographic skills?
    A stenographer should
        I. date her notebook daily to facilitate locating certain notes at a later time
        II. make corrections of grammatical mistakes while her boss is dictating to her
        III. draw a line through the dictated matter in her notebook after she has transcribed it
        IV. write in longhand unfamiliar names and addresses dictated to her
    The CORRECT answer is:

    A. I, II, III
    B. II, III, IV
    C. I, III, IV
    D. All of the above

25. A bureau of a city agency is about to move to a new location.
    Of the following, the FIRST step that should be taken in order to provide a good layout for the office at the new location is to

A. decide the exact amount of space to be assigned to each unit of the bureau
B. decide whether to lay out a single large open office or one consisting of small partitioned units
C. ask each unit chief in the bureau to examine the new location and submit a request for the amount of space he needs
D. prepare a detailed plan of the dimensions of the floor space to be occupied by the bureau at the new location

---

KEY (CORRECT ANSWERS)

1. A
2. B
3. B
4. C
5. A

6. A
7. D
8. B
9. A
10. D

11. A
12. D
13. A
14. B
15. A

16. C
17. B
18. C
19. C
20. B

21. B
22. D
23. C
24. C
25. D

TEST 2

DIRECTIONS: Each question or incomplete statement is followed by several suggested answers or completions. Select the one that BEST answers the question or completes the statement. *PRINT THE LETTER OF THE CORRECT ANSWER IN THE SPACE AT THE RIGHT.*

1. Suppose you are the supervisor of the mailroom of a large agency where the mail received daily is opened by machine, sorted by hand for delivery and time-stamped. Letters and any enclosures are removed from envelopes and stapled together before distribution. One of your newest clerks asks you what should be done when a letter makes reference to an enclosure, but no enclosure is in the envelope.
   You should tell him that in this situation the BEST procedure is to

   A. make an entry of the sender's name and address in the "missing enclosures" file and forward the letter to its proper destination
   B. return the letter to its sender, attaching a request for the missing enclosure
   C. put the letter aside until a proper investigation may be made concerning the missing enclosure
   D. route the letter to the person for whom it is intended, noting the absence of the enclosure on the letter margin

   1._____

2. The term "work flow," when used in connection with office management or the activities in an office, GENERALLY means the

   A. use of charts in the analysis of various office functions
   B. rate of speed at which work flows through a single section of an office
   C. step-by-step physical routing of work through its various procedures
   D. number of individual work units which can be produced by the average employee

   2._____

3. Physical conditions can have a definite effect on the efficiency and morale of an office. Which of the following statements about physical conditions in an office is CORRECT?

   A. Hard, non-porous surfaces reflect more noise than linoleum on the top of a desk.
   B. Painting in tints of bright yellow is more appropriate for sunny, well-lit offices than for dark, poorly-lit offices.
   C. Plate glass is better than linoleum for the top of a desk.
   D. The central typing room needs less light than a conference room does.

   3._____

4. In a certain filing system, documents are consecutively numbered as they are filed, a register is maintained of such consecutively numbered documents, and a record is kept of the number of each document removed from the files and its destination.
   This system will NOT help in

   A. finding the present whereabouts of a particular document
   B. proving the accuracy of the data recorded on a certain document
   C. indicating whether observed existing documents were ever filed
   D. locating a desired document without knowing what its contents are

   4._____

5. In deciding the kind and number of records an agency should keep, the administrative staff must recognize that records are of value in office management PRIMARILY as

   5._____

7

A. informational bases for agency activities
B. data for evaluating the effectiveness of the agency
C. raw material on which statistical analyses are to be based
D. evidence that the agency is carrying out its duties and responsibilities

6. Complaints are often made by the public about the city government's procedures. Although in most cases such procedures cannot be changed since various laws and regulations require them, it may still be possible to reduce the number of complaints. Which one of the following actions by personnel dealing with applicants for city services is LEAST likely to reduce complaints concerning city procedures?

    A. Treating all citizens alike and explaining to them that no exceptions to required procedures can be made
    B. Explaining briefly to the citizen why he should comply with regulations
    C. Being careful to avoid mistakes which may make additional interviews or correspondence necessary
    D. Keeping the citizen informed of the progress of his correspondence when immediate disposition cannot be made

7. In answering a complaint made by a member of the public that a certain essential procedure required by your agency is difficult to follow, it would be BEST for you to stress MOST

    A. that a change in the rules may be considered if enough complaints are received
    B. why the operation of a large agency sometimes proves a hardship in individual cases
    C. the necessity for the procedure
    D. the origin of the procedure

8. When talking to a citizen, it is BEST for an employee of government to

    A. use ordinary conversational phrases and a natural manner
    B. try to copy the pronunciation and level of education shown by the citizen
    C. try to speak in a very cultured manner and tone
    D. use technical terms to show his familiarity with his own work

9. Employees who service the public should maintain an attitude which is both sympathetic and objective.
An UNSYMPATHETIC and SUBJECTIVE attitude would be shown by a public employee who

    A. says "no" with a smile when a citizen's request must be denied
    B. listens attentively to a long complaint from a citizen about the government's "red tape"
    C. responds with sarcasm when a citizen asks a question which has an obvious answer
    D. suggests a definite solution to a citizen's problems

10. You are a supervisor in a city agency and are holding your first interview with a new employee.
In this interview, you should strive MAINLY to

A. show the new employee that you are an efficient and objective supervisor, with a completely impersonal attitude toward your subordinates
B. complete the entire orientation process including the giving of detailed job-duty instructions
C. make it clear to the employee that all your decisions are based on your many years of experience
D. lay the groundwork for a good employee-supervisor relationship by gaining the new employee's confidence

11. A senior clerk or senior typist may be required to help train a newly-appointed clerk. Which of the following is LEAST important for a newly-appointed clerk to know in order to perform his work efficiently?

    A. Acceptable ways of answering and recording telephone calls
    B. The number of files in the storage files unit
    C. The filing methods used by his unit
    D. Proper techniques for handling visitors

12. In your agency, you have the responsibility of processing clients who have appointments with agency representatives. On a particularly busy day, a client comes to your desk and insists that she must see the person handling her case although she has no appointment.
    Under the circumstances, your FIRST action should be to

    A. show her the full appointment schedule
    B. give her an appointment for another day
    C. ask her to explain the urgency
    D. tell her to return later in the day

13. Which of the following practices is BEST for a supervisor to use when assigning work to his staff?

    A. Give workers with seniority the most difficult jobs
    B. Assign all unimportant work to the slower workers
    C. Permit each employee to pick the job he prefers
    D. Make assignments based on the workers' abilities

14. In which of the following instances is a supervisor MOST justified in giving commands to people under his supervision? When

    A. they delay in following instructions which have been given to them clearly
    B. they become relaxed and slow about work, and he wants to speed up their production
    C. he must direct them in an emergency situation
    D. he is instructing them on jobs that are unfamiliar to them

15. Which of the following supervisory actions or attitudes is MOST likely to result in getting subordinates to try to do as much work as possible for a supervisor? He

    A. shows that his most important interest is in schedules and production goals
    B. consistently pressures his staff to get the work out
    C. never fails to let them know he is in charge
    D. considers their abilities and needs while requiring that production goals be met

16. Assume that a senior clerk has been explaining certain regulations to a new clerk under his supervision.
    The MOST efficient way for the senior clerk to make sure that the clerk has understood the explanation is to

    A. give him written materials on the regulations
    B. ask him if he has any further questions about the regulations
    C. ask him specific questions based on what has just been explained to him
    D. watch the way he handles a situation involving these regulations

17. One of your unit clerks has been assigned to work for a Mr. Jones in another office for several days. At the end of the first day, Mr. Jones, saying the clerk was not satisfactory, asks that she not be assigned to him again. This clerk is one of your most dependable workers, and no previous complaints about her work have come to you from any other outside assignments.
    To get to the root of this situation, your FIRST action should be to

    A. ask Mr. Jones to explain in what way her work was unsatisfactory
    B. ask the clerk what she did that Mr. Jones considered unsatisfactory
    C. check with supervisors for whom she previously worked to see if your own rating of her is in error
    D. tell Mr. Jones to pick the clerk he would prefer to have work for him the next time

18. A senior typist, still on probation, is instructed to type, as quickly as possible, one section of a draft of a long, complex report. Her part must be typed and readable before another part of the report can be written. Asked when she can have the report ready, she gives her supervisor an estimate of a day longer than she knows it will actually take. She then finishes the job a day sooner than the date given her supervisor.
    The judgment shown by a senior typist in giving an overestimate of time in a situation like this is, in general,

    A. *good,* because it prevents the supervisor from thinking she works slowly
    B. *good,* because it keeps unrealistic supervisors from expecting too much
    C. *bad,* because she should have used the time left to further check and proofread her work
    D. *bad,* because schedules and plans for other parts of the project may have been based on her false estimate

19. Suppose a new clerk, still on probation, is placed under your supervision and refuses to do a job you ask him to do.
    What is the FIRST thing you should do?

    A. Explain that you are the supervisor, and he must follow your instructions.
    B. Tell him he may be suspended if he refuses.
    C. Ask someone else to do the job, and rate him accordingly.
    D. Ask for his reason for objecting to the request.

20. As a supervisor of a small group of people, you have blamed worker A for something that you later find out was really done by worker B.
    The BEST thing for you to do now would be to

    A. say nothing to worker A, but criticize worker B for his mistake while worker A is near so that A will realize that you know who made the mistake
    B. speak to each worker separately, apologize to worker A for your mistake, and discuss worker B's mistake with him
    C. bring both workers together, apologize to worker A for your mistake, and discuss worker B's mistake with him
    D. say nothing new but be careful about mixing up worker A with worker B in the future

21. You have just learned one of your staff is grumbling that she thinks you are not pleased with her work. As far as you are concerned, this is not true at all. In fact, you have paid no particular attention to this worker lately because you have been very busy. You have just finished preparing an important report and "breaking in" a new clerk.
    Under the circumstances, the BEST thing to do is

    A. ignore her; after all, it is just a figment of her imagination
    B. discuss the matter with her now to try to find out and eliminate the cause of this problem
    C. tell her not to worry about it; you have not had time to think about her work
    D. make a note to meet with her at a later date in order to straighten out the situation

22. A most important job of a supervisor is to positively motivate employees to increase their work production. Which of the following LEAST indicates that a group of workers has been positively motivated?

    A. Their work output becomes constant and stable.
    B. Their cooperation at work becomes greater.
    C. They begin to show pride in the product of their work.
    D. They show increased interest in their work.

23. Which of the following traits would be LEAST important in considering a person for a merit increase?

    A. Punctuality
    B. Using initiative successfully
    C. High rate of production
    D. Resourcefulness

24. Of the following, the action LEAST likely to gain a supervisor the cooperation of his staff is for him to

    A. give each person consideration as an individual
    B. be as objective as possible when evaluating work performance
    C. rotate the least popular assignments
    D. expect subordinates to be equally competent

25. It has been said that, for the supervisor, nothing can beat the "face-to-face" communication of talking to one subordinate at a time.
    This method is, however, LEAST appropriate to use when the

    A. supervisor is explaining a change in general office procedure
    B. subject is of personal importance
    C. supervisor is conducting a yearly performance evaluation of all employees
    D. supervisor must talk to some of his employees concerning their poor attendance and punctuality

---

KEY (CORRECT ANSWERS)

1.	D	11.	B
2.	C	12.	C
3.	A	13.	D
4.	B	14.	C
5.	A	15.	D
6.	A	16.	C
7.	C	17.	A
8.	A	18.	D
9.	C	19.	D
10.	D	20.	B

21.	B
22.	A
23.	A
24.	D
25.	A

TEST 3

DIRECTIONS: Each question or incomplete statement is followed by several suggested answers or completions. Select the one that BEST answers the question or completes the statement. *PRINT THE LETTER OF THE CORRECT ANSWER IN THE SPACE AT THE RIGHT.*

1. While you are on the telephone answering a question about your agency, a visitor comes to your desk and starts to ask you a question. There is no emergency or urgency in either situation, that of the phone call or that of answering the visitor's question.
   In this case, you should

   1._____

   A. continue to answer the person on the telephone until you are finished and then tell the visitor you are sorry to have kept him waiting
   B. excuse yourself to the person on the telephone and tell the visitor that you will be with him as soon as you have finished on the phone
   C. explain to the person on the telephone that you have a visitor and must shorten the conversation
   D. continue to answer the person on the phone while looking up occasionally at the visitor to let him know that you know he is waiting

2. While speaking on the telephone to someone who called, you are disconnected.
   The FIRST thing you should do is

   2._____

   A. hang up, but try to keep your line free to receive the call back
   B. immediately get the dial tone and continually dial the person who called you until you reach him
   C. signal the switchboard operator and ask her to re-establish the connection
   D. dial "O" for Operator and explain that you were disconnected

3. The type of speech used by an office worker in telephone conversation greatly affects the communication.
   Of the following, the BEST way to express your ideas when telephoning is with a vocabulary that consists MAINLY of

   3._____

   A. formal, intellectual sounding words
   B. often used colloquial words
   C. technical, emphatic words
   D. simple, descriptive words

4. Suppose a clerk under your supervision has taken a personal phone call and is at the same time needed to answer a question regarding an assignment being handled by another member of your office. He appears confused as to what he should do. How should you instruct him later as to how to handle a similar situation?
   You should tell him to

   4._____

   A. tell the caller to hold on while he answers the question
   B. tell the caller to call back a little later
   C. return the call during an assigned break
   D. finish the conversation quickly and answer the question

5. You are asked to place a telephone call by your supervisor. When you place the call, you receive what appears to be a wrong number.
   Of the following, you should FIRST

   A. check the number with your supervisor to see if the number he gave you is correct
   B. ask the person on the other end what his number is and who he is
   C. check with the person on the other end to see if the number you dialed is the number you received
   D. apologize to the person on the other end for disturbing him and hang up

6. When you select someone to serve as supervisor of your unit during your absence on vacation and at other times, it would generally be BEST to choose the employee who is

   A. able to move the work along smoothly, without friction
   B. on staff longest
   C. liked best by the rest of the staff
   D. able to perform the work of each employee to be supervised

7. Successful supervision of handicapped persons employed in a department depends MOST on providing them with a work place and work climate

   A. which is safe and accident-free
   B. that requires close and direct supervision by others
   C. that requires the performance of routine, repetitive tasks under a minimum of pressure
   D. where they will be accepted by the other employees

8. Studies have indicated that when employees feel that their work is aimless and unchallenging, the allocation or payment of more money for this type of work is likely to

   A. contribute little to increased production
   B. bring more status to this work
   C. increase employees' feelings of security
   D. give employees greater motivation

9. An employee's performance has fallen below established minimum standards of quantity and quality.
   The threat of monetary or other disciplinary action as a device for improving this employee's performance would probably be acceptable and MOST effective

   A. only if applied as soon as the performance fell below standard
   B. only after more constructive techniques have failed
   C. at any time provided the employee understands that the punishment will be carried out
   D. at no time

10. A supervisor must, on short notice, ask his staff to work overtime.
    Of the following, a technique that is MOST likely to win their willing cooperation would be to

    A. explain that occasional overtime is part of the job requirement
    B. explain that they will be doing him a personal favor which he will appreciate very much

C. explain why the overtime is necessary
D. promise them that they can take the extra time off in the near future

11. On checking a completed work assignment of an employee, the supervisor finds that the work was not done correctly because the employee had not understood his instructions. Of the following, the BEST way to prevent repetition of this situation next time is for the supervisor to

    A. ask the employee whether he fully understood the instructions and tell him to ask questions in the future whenever anything is unclear
    B. ask the employee to repeat the instructions given and test his understanding with several key questions
    C. give the instructions a second time, emphasizing the more complicated aspects of the job
    D. give work instructions in writing

12. If, as a supervisor, you find yourself pressured for time to handle all of your job responsibilities, the one of the following tasks which it would be MOST appropriate for you to delegate to a subordinate is

    A. attending a staff conference of unit supervisors to discuss the implementation of a new departmental policy
    B. making staff work assignments
    C. interviewing a new employee
    D. checking work of certain employees for accuracy

13. Suppose you are unavoidably late for work one morning. When you arrive at 10 o'clock, you find there are several matters demanding your attention.
    Which one of the following matters should you handle LAST?

    A. A visitor who had a 9:30 appointment with you has been waiting to see you since 9 o'clock.
    B. An employee on an assignment which should have been completed that morning is absent, and the work will have to be reassigned.
    C. Several letters which you dictated at the end of the previous day have been typed and are on your desk for signature and mailing.
    D. Your superior called asking you to get certain information for him when you come in and to call him back.

14. Suppose that you have assigned a typist to type a report containing considerable statistical and tabular material and have given her specific instructions as to how this material is to be laid out on each page. When she returns the completed report, you find that it was not prepared according to your instructions, but you may possibly be able to use it the way it was typed. When you question her, she states that she thought her layout was better but you were unavailable for consultation when she began the work.
    Of the following, the BEST action for you to take is to

    A. criticize her for not doing the work according to your instructions
    B. have her retype the report
    C. praise her for her work but tell her she should have waited until she could consult you
    D. praise her for using initiative

15. Of the following, the MOST effective way for a supervisor to correct poor work habits of an employee which result in low and poor quality output is to give the employee

    A. additional training
    B. less demanding assignments until his work improves
    C. continuous supervision
    D. more severe criticism

16. Of the following, the BEST way for a supervisor to teach an employee how to do a new and somewhat complicated job is to

    A. assign him to observe another employee who is already skilled in this work and instruct him to consult this employee if he has any questions
    B. explain to him how to do it, then demonstrate how it is done, then observe and correct the employee as he does it, then follow up
    C. give him a written, detailed, step-by-step explanation of how to do the job and instruct him to ask questions if anything is unclear when he does the work
    D. teach him the easiest part of the job first, then the other parts one at a time, in order of their difficulty, as the employee masters the easier parts

17. After an employee has completed telling his supervisor about a grievance against a co-worker, the supervisor tells the employee that he will take action to remove the cause of the grievance.
    The action of the supervisor was

    A. *good,* because ill feeling between subordinates interferes with proper performance
    B. *poor,* because the supervisor should give both employees time to "cool off"
    C. *good,* because grievances that appear petty to the supervisor are important to subordinates
    D. *poor,* because the supervisor should tell the employee that he will investigate the matter before he comes to any conclusion

18. During work on an important project, one employee in a secretarial pool turns in several pages of typed copy, one page of which contains several errors.
    Of these four comments which her supervisor might possibly make, which one would be MOST constructive?

    A. "You did such a poor job on this; I will have to have it done over."
    B. "You will have to do better, more consistently than this, if you want to be in charge of a secretarial pool yourself someday."
    C. "How come you made so many mistakes here? Your other pages were all right."
    D. "If my boss saw this, he would be very displeased with you."

19. A supervisor has general supervision over a large, complex project with many employees. The work is subdivided among small units of employees, each with a senior clerk or senior stenographer in charge. At a staff meeting, after all work assignments have been made, the supervisor tells all the employees that they are to take orders only from their immediate supervisor and instructs them to let him know if anyone else tries to give them orders.
    This instruction by the supervising clerk is

A. *good,* because it may prevent the issuance of orders by unauthorized persons, which would interfere with the accomplishment of the assignment
B. *poor,* because employees should be instructed to take up such problems with their immediate supervisor
C. *good,* because orders issued by immediate supervisors would be precise and directly related to the tasks of the assignments while those issued by others would not be
D. *poor,* because it places upon all employees a responsibility which should not normally be theirs

20. A supervisor who is to direct a team of senior clerks and clerks in a complex project, calls them together beforehand to inform them of the tasks each employee will perform on this job.
Of the following, the CHIEF value of this action by the supervisor is that each member of this team will be able to

    A. work independently in the absence of the supervisor
    B. understand what he will do and how this will fit into the total picture
    C. share in the process of decision-making as an equal participant
    D. judge how well the plans for this assignment have been made

21. A supervisor who has both younger and older employees under his supervision may sometimes find that employee absenteeism seriously interferes with accomplishment of goals.
Studies of such employee absenteeism have shown that the absences of employees

    A. under 35 years of age are usually unexpected and the absences of employees over 45 years of age are usually unnecessary
    B. of all age groups show the same characteristics as to length of absence
    C. under 35 years of age are for frequent, short periods while the absences of employees over 45 years of age are less frequent but of longer duration
    D. under 35 years of age are for periods of long duration and the absences of employees over 45 years of age are for periods of short duration

22. Suppose you have a long-standing procedure for getting a certain job done by your subordinates that is apparently a good one. Changes in some steps of the procedure are made from time to time to handle special problems that come up.
For you to review this procedure periodically is desirable MAINLY because

    A. the system is working well
    B. checking routines periodically is a supervisor's chief responsibility
    C. subordinates may be confused as to how the procedure operates as a result of the changes made
    D. it is necessary to determine whether the procedure has become outdated or is in need of improvement

23. Suppose that a stranger enters the office you are in charge of and asks for the address and telephone number of one of your employees.
Of the following, it would be BEST for you to

    A. find out why he needs the information and release it if his reason is a good one
    B. explain that you are not permitted to release such information to unauthorized persons

C. give him the information but tell him it must be kept confidential
D. ask him to leave the office immediately

24. A member of the public approaches an employee who is at work at his desk. The employee cannot interrupt his work in order to take care of this person.
Of the following, the BEST and MOST courteous way of handling this situation is for the employee to

A. avoid looking up from his work until he is finished with what he is doing
B. tell this person that he will not be able to take care of him for quite a while
C. refer the individual to another employee who can take care of him right away
D. chat with the individual while he continues with his work

25. You answer a phone call from a citizen who urgently needs certain information you do not have, but you think you know who may have it. He is angry because he has already been switched to two different offices.
Of the following, it would be BEST for you to

A. give him the phone number of the person you think may have the information he wants, but explain you are not sure
B. tell him you regret you cannot help him because you are not sure who can give him the information
C. advise him that the best way he can be sure of getting the information he wants is to write a letter to the agency
D. get the phone number where he can be reached and tell him you will try to get the information he wants and will call him back later

KEY (CORRECT ANSWERS)

1. B
2. A
3. D
4. C
5. C

6. A
7. D
8. A
9. B
10. C

11. B
12. D
13. C
14. A
15. A

16. B
17. D
18. C
19. B
20. B

21. C
22. D
23. B
24. C
25. D

EXAMINATION SECTION
TEST 1

DIRECTIONS: Each question or incomplete statement is followed by several suggested answers or completions. Select the one that BEST answers the question or completes the statement. *PRINT THE LETTER OF THE CORRECT ANSWER IN THE SPACE AT THE RIGHT.*

1. The new head of a central filing unit, after studying a procedure in use, decided that it was unsatisfactory. He thereupon drew up an entirely new procedure which made no use of and ignored the existing procedure.
   This plan of action is, in general,
   A. *satisfactory*; a new broom sweeps clean
   B. *unsatisfactory*; any plan should use available resources to the utmost before resorting to new creation
   C. *satisfactory*; in general, use of part of an old procedure and part of a new procedure results sin an unworkable patchwork arrangement
   D. *unsatisfactory*; before deciding that the existing procedure was unusable, he should have requested that an independent, unbiased agency study the problem
   E. *satisfactory*; it is usually less time consuming to construct a new plan than to remedy an old one

1.____

2. Assume that you have broken a complex job into simpler and smaller components.
   After you have assigned a component to each employee, should you proceed to teach each employee a number of alternative methods for doing his job?
   A. *yes*; the more methods for performing a job an employee knows, the more chance there is that he will choose the one best suited to his abilities
   B. *No*; experienced employees should be permitted to decide how to perform the jobs assigned to them
   C. *Yes*; if several different methods are available, a desirable flexibility of operation results
   D. *No*; a single method for each job should be decided upon and taught
   E. *Yes*; the employees will have greater interest in their jobs

2.____

3. Assume that you are the head of a major staff unit and that a line unit has requested from your unit a special report to be completed in one day. After reviewing the request, you decide that much tie would be saved if two items which you know are superfluous are omitted from the report. You discuss the matter with the head of the other unit and he still insists that the two items are essential for his purposes.
   The one of the following actions which you should take at this stage is to
   A. plan to complete the report, including the two items, as expeditiously as possible
   B. write a memorandum to the department head giving both opinions fairly and asking for a decision

3.____

C. plan to complete the report without the two items, as expeditiously as possible
D. devise a plan for preparing the report without the two items which will permit you to add them later if they prove necessary although some time may be lost
E. again review the report with the line unit showing them why the two items are unnecessary

4. The one of the following functions of a supervisor which can be MOST successfully delegated is
   A. responsibility for accomplishing the unit's mission
   B. handling discipline
   C. checking completed work
   D. reporting to the bureau chief
   E. placing subordinates in the proper job

5. It is a standard operating procedure in an office which receives several thousand forms each week to have the file on clerk accumulate a week's receipts before filing them. The forms will not be examined for a period of one month after receipt.
   In comparison with daily filing, this procedure is, in general,
   A. *less satisfactory*; it keeps the files unnecessarily incomplete
   B. *more satisfactory*; it tends to reduce filing time
   C. *less satisfactory*; all information should be placed in a safe storage place as soon as possible
   D. *more satisfactory*; it tends to eliminate the prefiling period
   E. *less satisfactory*; it tends to build up an unnecessary period

6. Some organizations attempt to keep a constant backlog of work.
   This procedure is usually
   A. *undesirable*; reports are not ready when they are needed
   B. *desirable*; it tends to insure continuity of work flow
   C. *undesirable*; production records are too difficult to keep
   D. *desirable*; it tends to keep the employees under constant pressure
   E. *undesirable*; it tends to keep the employees under constant pressure

7. The first few times a procedure is carried through, a close check should be kept of all work times.
   The PRIMARY reason for this is to
   A. be able to present a clear picture of the situation
   B. determine if the employees understand the procedure
   C. evaluate the efficiency which may have been presented by the new procedure
   D. determine the efficiency of the employees
   E. permit revision of schedules

8. The one of the following pieces of information which is of LEAST importance in setting up the schedule for a given job is the time
   A. which is required to perform each component of the job
   B. when the source material will be available
   C. the job will take under adverse conditions
   D. by which the job must be completed
   E. employees will be available

9. Every employee should have a thorough knowledge of the organization of which he is a part.
   Of the following, the BEST justification for the above opinion is that
   A. the feeling of being a member of a team develops a responsible attitude toward one's everyday duties
   B. in an emergency, an employee may be called upon to perform duties other than his own
   C. the intricate details of an organization as complicated as a city department cannot easily be reduced to an organization chart
   D. an understanding of the different specialized units in an organization is often necessary to achieve the organization's given objective
   E. many city jobs are technical; thus, each employee should be trained to have more than a single narrow skill

10. The one of the following which is NOT a good rule in administering discipline is for you as a supervisor to
    A. reprimand the employee in private even though the fault was committed before others
    B. allow the employee a chance to reply to your criticism if he wishes
    C. be as specific as possible in criticizing the employee for his faults
    D. be sure you have all the facts before you reprimand an employee for an error he has committed
    E. allow an extended period to elapse after an error has been committed before reprimanding an employee

11. After you have submitted your annual evaluations of the work of your subordinates, one of them whose work has not been satisfactory complains to you that your evaluation was unjustified.
    For you to avoid discussing the evaluation but to point out two or three specific instances where the employee's work was below standard is
    A. *desirable*; an employee should be told what aspects of his work are unsatisfactory
    B. *undesirable*; once the evaluation has been submitted, there is no point in reconsidering it
    C. *desirable*; once the evaluation has been submitted, there is no point in reconsidering it but a discussion of the employee's weaknesses may help
    D. *undesirable*; it would have been better to explain how you arrived at your evaluation
    E. *desirable*; entering into a general argument is bad for the discipline of an organization

12. The chief of a central files bureau which has 50 employees customarily spends a considerable portion of his time in spot-checking the files, reviewing material being transferred from active to inactive files and similar activities.
From the viewpoint of the department top management, the MOST pertinent evaluation which can be made on the basis of this information is that the
    A. supervisor is conscientious and hardworking
    B. bureau may need additional staff
    C. supervisor has not made a sufficient delegation of authority and responsibility
    D. bureau needs an in-service training course as the work of its employees requires an abnormal amount of review
    E. filing system employed may be inadequate

12._____

13. Assume that you are in charge of a unit with 40 employees. The department head requests immediate preparation of a special and rather complicated report which will take about a day to complete if everyone in your unit works on it.
After breaking the job into simple components and assigning each component to an employee, should more than one person be instructed on the procedure to be followed on each component?
    A. *No*; the procedure would be a waste of time in this instance
    B. *Yes*; it is always desirable to have a replacement available in the event of illness or any other emergency
    C. *No*; in general, as long as an employee's job performance is satisfactory, there is no need to train an alternate
    D. *Yes*; the presence of more than one person in a unit who can perform a given task tends to prevent the formation of a bottleneck
    E. *No*; there is, in general, no need to train more than one employee in the performance of a special job

13._____

14. A new employee who has shown that she is capable of performing superior work during the first month of her employment falls far below this standard after the first month.
For the supervisor to wait until the end of the probationary period and then recommend that she be discharged if her work is still unsatisfactory is
    A. *undesirable*; she should have been discharged when her work became unsatisfactory
    B. *desirable*; there is no place in the civil service for unsatisfactory employees
    C. *undesirable*; he should immediately attempt to determine the cause of the poor performance
    D. *desirable*; the employee is entitled to an opportunity to prove herself
    E. *undesirable*; the employee is obviously capable of performing good work and simply requires some guidance from the supervisor

14._____

15. In order to make sure that work is completed on time, the unit supervisor should
    A. use the linear method of delegating responsibility
    B. pitch in and do as much of the work himself as he can
    C. schedule the work and keep himself informed of its progress
    D. not assign more than one person to any one task
    E. know the capabilities of his subordinates

15.____

16. One of the more effective ways to obtain optimum performance from employees is to keep them off balance by not letting them feel secure in the job; to permit an employee to feel secure is to invite him to settle into a comfortable rut.
    The point of view expressed in this statement is
    A. *correct*; studies have shown that the degree of effort put forth on a job generally varies directly with the degree of job insecurity
    B. *incorrect*; studies have shown that a relatively high degree of security is conducive to best job performance
    C. *correct*; while studies have shown that there is little relationship between security and job performance, what tendencies are present to support the point of view expressed
    D. *incorrect*; studies have shown that there is little relationship between security and job performance and what tendencies are present are opposed to the point of view expressed
    E. *correct*; while no specific studies have been made in this field, analogous studies made in similar fields show that permitting a feeling of security to develop results in decreased job performance

16.____

Questions 17-19.

DIRECTIONS: Questions 17 through 19 are to be answered on the basis of the following paragraph.

The supervisor of a large clerical and statistical division has assigned to one of the units under his supervision the preparation of a special statistical report required by the department head. The unit accepted the assignment without comment but soon ran into considerable difficulty because no one in his unit had had any statistical training.

17. If a result of this lack of training is that the report is not completed on time, although everyone has done all that could be expected, the responsibility for the failure rests with
    A. the department head   B. the supervisor
    C. the unit head   D. the employees in the unit
    E. no one

17.____

18. This incident indicates that the supervisory staff has insufficient knowledge of employee
    A. capabilities
    B. reaction to increased demands
    C. on-the-job training needs
    D. work habits
    E. ability to perform ordinary assignments

18.____

19. After working on the report for two days, the unit head notifies the supervisor that he will not be able to get the report out in the required time. He states that his staff will be completely trained in another day or two and that after preparing the report will be a simple matter. At this stage, the supervisor decides to have the statistical unit prepare the report.
    This action on the part of the supervisor is
    A. *undesirable*; the unit head should be given an incentive to continue with his training program which may produce good results
    B. *desirable*; it is the most effective way in which the supervisor can show his displeasure with the unit head's failure
    C. *undesirable*; it may adversely affect the morale of the unit
    D. *desirable*; it will generally result in a better report completed in a shorter time
    E. *undesirable*; the time spent training the unit will be completely wasted

19.____

20. A supervisor criticizes a subordinate's work by telling him that he is disappointed with it. The supervisor states that the work is completely unsatisfactory, shows where it is bad, and says that improvement is expected.
    This approach is usually
    A. *good*; the employee knows just where he stands
    B. *poor*; some favorable comment should be made at the same time if possible
    C. *good*; it is good policy to keep this type of interview as short as possible
    D. *poor*; the employee should be asked to explain why his work is poor
    E. *good*; the supervisor did not criticize the subordinate in front of other employees

20.____

Questions 21-25.

DIRECTIONS: Column I below lists five kinds of statistical data which are to be transformed into a chart or a graph for incorporation into the department annual report. Column II lists nine different kinds of graphs or charts. For each type of information listed in Column I, select the chart or graph from Column II by means of which it should be demonstrated.

COLUMN I

21. The relationship between employees' occupational classification and their salaries, for all employees by occupational classification, showing minimum, maximum, and average salary in each group.

22. A comparison of the number of employees in the department, the departmental budget the number of employees in the operating divisions and the operating division budget for each year over a ten-year period.

COLUMN II

A. [horizontal bar chart]

B. [pie chart]

C. [vertical bar chart]

21.____

22.____

COLUMN I	COLUMN II	
23. The amount of money spent for each of the department's 10 most important functions during the past year.	D. 	23._____
24. The percentage of the department's budget spent for each of the department's activities for each year over a ten-year period.	E. 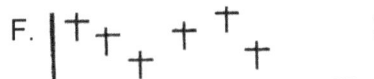	24._____
25. The number of each kind of employee employed in the department over a period of twenty years and the total number of employees in the department for each of these periods.	F. 	25._____
	G. 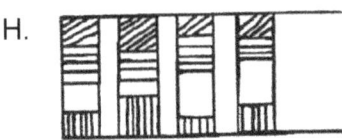	
	H. 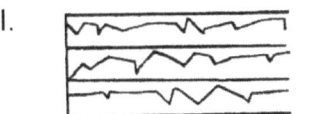	
	I.	

KEY (CORRECT ANSWERS)

1.	B	11.	D
2.	D	12.	C
3.	A	13.	A
4.	C	14.	C
5.	B	15.	C
6.	B	16.	B
7.	E	17.	B
8.	C	18.	A
9.	A	19.	D
10.	E	20.	B

21. F
22. D
23. C
24. H
25. G

TEST 2

DIRECTIONS: Each question or incomplete statement is followed by several suggested answers or completions. Select the one that BEST answers the question or completes the statement. *PRINT THE LETTER OF THE CORRECT ANSWER IN THE SPACE AT THE RIGHT.*

1. The report of the head of Unit Y to his bureau chief on the performance of a new clerical employee indicates that the performance is not up to the expected standard. After reading the report, the bureau chief transferred the employee to Unit X.
   This action on the part of the bureau chief was
   A. in line with good personal practice; an employee who does poorly in one place may do better in another
   B. premature; an attempt to discover the cause of the poor performance should be made first
   C. desirable; personnel reports become meaningless unless acted upon at once
   D. undesirable; unsatisfactory employees should be dismissed and not transferred from unit to unit
   E. in the best interest of the organization; whenever a supervisor cannot get along with a subordinate for whatever reason, it is desirable to transfer the subordinate

   1.____

2. Suppose that you have been consulted by a department head who wishes to initiate an in-service training course in his department. The department head suggests that, as a first step, a training course be initiated for supervisors in the department.
   This suggestion is BEST characterized as
   A. *undesirable*; the supervisors are generally the persons least in need of work incentives
   B. *desirable*; it is generally cheaper and more effective to train a few supervisors than a large number of employees
   C. *undesirable*; supervisors may be held up to ridicule if they are isolated for training
   D. *desirable*; trained supervisors are needed to train employees
   E. *undesirable*; employees should be trained before supervisors

   2.____

3. Any person thoroughly familiar with the specific steps in a particular class of work is well qualified to serve as a training course instructor in that work.
   This statement is erroneous CHIEFLY because
   A. it is practically impossible for any instructor to be acquainted with all the specific steps sin a particular class of work
   B. what is true of one class of work is not necessarily true of other types of work
   C. a qualified instructor cannot be expected to have detailed information about many specific fields

   3.____

27

D. the steps in any type of work are usually interrelated and not independent or unique
E. the quantity of information possessed by an instructor does not bear a direct relationship to the quality of instruction

4. Of the following, the MOST significant argument against making it compulsory for civil service employees to attend a training course is that
    A. unwilling trainees will be penalized in any event by non-promotion
    B. most training requires additional time and expense on the part of the trainee
    C. training is highly desirable but not absolutely essential for adequate job performance
    D. incompetent work is generally reflected in poor service ratings
    E. trainees must be receptive if training is to be successful

5. There are four basic systems of job evaluation which have been extensively used by government and industry.
    The one of the following which is NOT one of these is the _____ system.
    A. Benchmark
    B. Factor Comparison
    C. Point
    D. Job Classification
    E. Ranking

6. Of the following, the CHIEF advantage derived by filling all vacancies in an organization by promotion from below rather than from outside the organization is that such a procedure
    A. fills existing vacancies from the widest possible recruitment base
    B. stimulates individual employees to improve their work habits
    C. avoids personality difficulties likely to arise when an employee is assigned to supervise former colleagues
    D. indirectly coordinates the work of different units by interchange of personnel
    E. encourages reorientation and review of administrative procedures

7. Of the following, the CHIEF justification for a periodic classification audit is that
    A. salaries should be readjusted at frequent intervals
    B. some degree of personnel turnover should always be expected
    C. a career service requires regular promotion opportunities
    D. employees require frequent stimulation and encouragement
    E. positions frequently change over a period of time

8. A classification analyst sorts jobs horizontally and vertically.
    Of the following, the LEAST important job factor to be considered with respect to vertical placement is
    A. independence of action and decision
    B. consequence of errors
    C. kind and character of work performed
    D. degree of supervision received
    E. determination of policy

3 (#2)

9. Assume that you have been assigned to prepare a plan for conducting a large scale job classification survey.
   Of the following, the BEST suggestion for reducing the number of appeals from the final allocations likely to be received after the classification study has been completed is to
   A. have supervisors check statements of employees on classification questionnaires
   B. allocate present positions to proposed classes according to jurisdictional assignments
   C. adjust salary to present level of work performed by employees
   D. allow employee participation throughout the classification process
   E. postpone controversial problems until simpler problems have been solved and a general blueprint laid down

9._____

10. A comment made by an employee about a training course was, *Oh, I suppose it's important for the job but it's a waste of time for me just to sit in that course and yawn while the instructor rambles on."*
    The fundamental error in training methodology to which this criticism points is failure to provide
    A. goals for the students
    B. for individual differences
    C. connecting links between new and old material
    D. for student participation
    E. motivation for the subject matter of the course

10._____

11. You are preparing a long report addressed to your superior on a study which you have conducted for him.
    The one of the following sections which should come FIRST in the report is a
    A. description of the working procedure utilized in the study
    B. description of the situation which exists
    C. summary of the conclusions of the survey
    D. discussion of possible objections to the report and their refutation
    E. description of the method of installing the recommendations

11._____

12. While setting up a reporting system to help the department planning section, an administrator proposed the policy that no overlap or duplication be permitted even if it meant that some minor areas were left uncovered.
    This policy is
    A. *undesirable*; overlap is frequently necessary
    B. *desirable*; the presence of overlap and duplication indicates defective planning
    C. *undesirable*; setting up general policy in advance of the specific reporting system may lead to inflexibility
    D. *desirable*; it is not necessary to get complete coverage in order to be able to plan operations
    E. *undesirable*; duplication is preferable to leaving any area uncovered

12._____

Questions 13-15.

DIRECTIONS: Questions 13 through 15 are to be answered on the basis of the following paragraph.

Prior to revising its child care program, a department feels that it is necessary to get some information from the mothers served by the existing program in order to determine where changes are required. A questionnaire is to be constructed to obtain this information.

13. Of the following points which can be taken into consideration in the construction of the questionnaire, the one which is of LEAST importance is
    A. that the data are to be put into punch cards
    B. the aspects of the program which seem to be in need of change
    C. the type of person who will fill out the questionnaire
    D. testing the questionnaire for ambiguity in advance of general distribution
    E. setting up a control group so that answers received can be compared to a standard

14. To discuss this questionnaire with all mothers who have been asked to answer it, before they actually fill it out, is
    A. *desirable*; the mothers may be able to offer valuable suggestions for changes in the form of the questionnaire
    B. *undesirable*; it is of some value but consumes too much valuable time
    C. *desirable*; cooperation and uniform interpretation will tend to be achieved
    D. *undesirable*; it may cause the answers to be biased
    E. *desirable*; the group will tend to support the program

15. Of the following items included in the questionnaire, the one which will be of LEAST assistance for comparing attitudes toward the program among different kinds of persons is
    A. name
    B. address
    C. age
    D. place of birth
    E. education

16. You have been asked, to prepare for public distribution, a statement dealing with a controversial matter.
    Of the following approaches, the one which would usually be MOST effective is to present your department's point of view
    A. as tersely as possible with no reference to any other matters
    B. developed from ideas and facts well known to most readers
    C. and show all the statistical data and techniques which were used in arriving at it
    D. in such a way that the controversial parts are omitted
    E. substantiated by supporting quotations from persons in the specialized field even if they are not well known

5 (#2)

17. During a conference of administrative staff personnel, the department head discussing the letter prepared for his signature stated, *"Use no more words than are necessary to express your meaning."*
Following this rule in letter writing is, in general,
   A. *desirable*; considerable time will be saved in the preparation of correspondence
   B. *undesirable*; it is frequently necessary to elaborate on an explanation in order to make certain that the reader will understand
   C. *desirable*; terse statements give government letters a business-like air which impresses readers favorably
   D. *undesirable*; terse statements are generally cold and formal and produce an unfavorable reaction in the reader
   E. *desirable*; the use of more words than are necessary is likely to obscure the meaning and tire the reader

17.____

18. While you are designing the layout for a departmental procedure manual, it is suggested that you carefully arrange your reading material so that there will be a minimum amount of blank space on the page.
Of the following judgments of this suggestion, the one which is the MOST valid basis for action is that it is
   A. *bad*; readability and ease of reference will be decreased
   B. *good*; the cost of production can be decreased considerably without any great disadvantage
   C. *of little or no importance*; more or less blank space on the page will not affect the value of the manual
   D. *good*; it will make for a smaller, easier to handle book
   E. *bad*; replacement of outdated pages is made more difficult by having more material on a page

18.____

19. After the planning of an employee's procedure manual had been completed, the suggestion was made that the manual should be prepared and arranged so that changes could be made readily.
Of the following decisions with respect to this suggestion, the one which is MOST desirable from the viewpoint of good administration is that the suggestions should
   A. not be considered as it is generally impossible to prepare a satisfactory manual which will take everything into consideration
   B. be followed only if it does not conflict with the planned layout
   C. be used even if it is somewhat more costly than the planned layout
   D. be noted and acted upon at the next revision of the manual
   E. not be considered as this type of manual is more difficult to maintain properly

19.____

20. Assume that you are in charge of preparing a procedure manual of about 100 pages for a large clerical unit. After you have decided to use a looseleaf format, one of your subordinates proposes that only one side of the page be printed.

20.____

This proposal is
- A. *good*; replacement of obsolete pages is made easier
- B. *poor*; cost is increased
- C. *good*; provision is automatically made for employee's notes
- D. *poor*; it will increase the size of the manual, making it more difficult to use
- E. *good*; indexing will be made easier

21. It may be assumed that if all departments had qualified personnel officers, not all departments would be lacking adequate training programs. However, the most cursory examination of the situation will show that some departments do not have adequate training programs. Thus, we must conclude that some of them lack qualified personnel officers.
    The argument presented in the report is
    - A. *correct*; the conclusion follows logically from the assumption and the facts
    - B. *not correct*; what can be concluded is that no department has a qualified personnel officer
    - C. *not correct*; no conclusion with respect to the presence of personnel officers in departments can be drawn from the information
    - D. *not correct*; what can be concluded is that the absence of an adequate training program in a department implies the absence of a personnel officer
    - E. *correct*; but the conclusion is false as the hypothesis is not true

22. In a study of the relationship between a fixed discipline policy and the incidence of lateness, it would be MOST informative to have data proving the statement:
    - A. In those organizations in which there are no fixed discipline policy, the incidence of lateness is variable.
    - B. The incidence of lateness has not decreased in those organizations where fixed discipline policies have been abandoned.
    - C. The incidence of lateness and the discipline policy vary from organization to organization.
    - D. Discipline policies sometimes ignore the problem of lateness.
    - E. In organizations with a fixed discipline policy, the incidence of lateness is variable.

23. The data prove that an increase in the number of clerks performing filing work results in an increased cost per item filed.
    On the basis of these data, we can be certain that
    - A. if filing costs per item filed increase, it is caused by an increase in the number of clerks filing
    - B. if filing costs per item filed decrease, the number of clerks filing cannot be increasing
    - C. if the number of clerks filing is changed, the unit cost per filing will change
    - D. if the number of clerks filing is not increased, the cost per unit filed will not increase
    - E. if the number of clerks filing is decreased, the cost per item filed will decrease

24. Each unit either has sufficient space assigned to it or it has not. No unit which has insufficient space assigned to it has neglected to ask for additional space. From these data, we can state
    A. units with sufficient space have not asked for additional space
    B. only units which have sufficient space have not asked for additional space
    C. nothing about the relationship between the need for additional space and requests made for additional space
    D. all units which have requested additional space have insufficient space
    E. no units which have requested additional space have sufficient space

24._____

25. One argument which is presented against a strict career system in the civil service is as follows:
    The employees who are recruited today for low-level jobs become the administrators of tomorrow. At the present time the employees we are attracting for the low-level jobs are untrained and poorly educated. Thus, it follows that the administrators of tomorrow will be untrained and poorly educated.
    The one of the following which is a CORRECT criticism of the reasoning is that
    A. the argument is logically correct but the conclusion is false as the hypothesis that we are attracting untrained and poorly educated people for our low-level job is false
    B. the conclusion does not follow logically from hypotheses
    C. the argument is logically correct, but the conclusion is false because it is a false hypothesis that tomorrow's administrators will come from employees who hold low-level jobs
    D. the argument is logically correct and the conclusion is correct
    E. while the argument is logically correct and the hypotheses are not demonstrably false, the argument ignores the realities of the case that those who are untrained today may be trained tomorrow

25._____

KEY (CORRECT ANSWERS)

1. B
2. D
3. E
4. E
5. A

6. B
7. E
8. C
9. D
10. D

11. C
12. E
13. E
14. C
15. A

16. B
17. E
18. A
19. C
20. A

21. C
22. B
23. B
24. B
25. B

TEST 3

DIRECTIONS: Each question or incomplete statement is followed by several suggested answers or completions. Select the one that BEST answers the question or completes the statement. *PRINT THE LETTER OF THE CORRECT ANSWER IN THE SPACE AT THE RIGHT.*

1. Surveying modern administration, it becomes clear that there is GREATEST need at present for administrators with
    A. a good knowledge of personnel administration
    B. the ability to write good reports
    C. a working knowledge of modern methods analysis
    D. a broad rather than specialized viewpoint
    E. the ability to analyze complicated fiscal programs

1._____

2. The one of the following which is a fundamental obstacle to effective planning in MOST governmental agencies is
    A. inadequate staff or resources
    B. the absence of the properly centralized administration
    C. the absence of clearly defined objective and constituent programs
    D. the neglect of analysis of ways and means
    E. the absence of functional boundaries for units and individuals

2._____

3. A department consists of several independent bureaus, each responsible to the commissioner for its own planning, operation, and reporting, a central personnel unit and the commissioner's office consisting of a secretary and several clerks to handle public relations.
The one of the following *undesirable* characteristics which is MOST likely to arise in this organization is
    A. absence of planning
    B. weak and ineffectual leadership
    C. failure to have employees properly trained
    D. a lack of an easily understandable goal
    E. duplication of work

3._____

4. The one of the following practices which is MOST likely to lead to confusion, recrimination and jurisdictional conflict among the bureaus of a department is the failure to
    A. make clear and unambiguous assignments
    B. systematically subdivide the work
    C. explain general policy to those responsible for its achievement
    D. allocate equitably available resources
    E. set up uniform operating procedures for all units

4._____

5. The one of the following which is MOST likely to occur in an over-specialized administrative set-up is
    A. inability to recruit proper personnel to fill over-specialized positions
    B. improper supervision
    C. failure of employees to realize the broad implications of their work

5._____

35

2 (#3)

    D. lack of proper decentralization of authority, as emphasis on specialization goes hand-in-hand with over-centralization
    E. inability to solve technical problems which are not entirely in one specialty

6. Of the following, the LEAST valid reason for a department head continuing to require that a weekly report be forwarded to him, is that the report forms a basis for
    A. measuring performance
    B. making decisions
    C. revising policy
    D. the execution of the mission of the unit which receives it
    E. the operation of the unit which is required to prepare it

6.____

7. Administrators must learn not to farm out essential functions to unintegrated agencies, but to organize all responsibilities in unified but decentralized hierarchies.
A problem which an administrator may be expected to face if he has not learned this is that
    A. the organization fails to develop administrators capable of independent action
    B. issues will not be posed at the level where decisions should be made
    C. relationships with the public will not be satisfactory
    D. it will be difficult to achieve administrative control or get agreement on departmental action
    E. individual agencies will be unable to complete the work scheduled

7.____

8. The central staff planning unit within any organization includes in its functions helping to plan policy at one extreme and planning detailed execution at the other extreme.
With respect to the actual execution, the planning activity should
    A. have no concern with it
    B. simply forward and explain new plans
    C. have only the responsibility of explaining in the form of plans the objectives of top management
    D. keep track of how the plans are working out but make no attempt to supervise their execution
    E. supervise the execution of new plans

8.____

9. The head of a department assigned final responsibility for the training function to the personnel office.
This assignment was
    A. *undesirable*; this type of centralization prevents a staff organization from carrying out staff functions
    B. *desirable*; experience has shown that centralization of this type results in more efficient and economic operation
    C. *undesirable*; the personnel office usually does not have the technical "know how" to carry this responsibility
    D. *desirable*; if training is left to the line officials, it never is accomplished
    E. *undesirable*; this responsibility must rest with the supervisor

9.____

10. A department head insisted that operating officials participate in the development of new procedures along with the planning section.
Participation of this type is, on the whole,
    A. *desirable*; operating realities are more likely to be considered
    B. *undesirable*; the inclusion of conflicting views before the plan is drawn may result in no plan
    C. *desirable*; plans will be more flexible and objectives more clearly defined
    D. *undesirable*; the operating officials should decide to what extent they wish to participate with no pressure from the top
    E. *desirable*; to back down on a procedure once it has been decided upon is a sign of weakness

11. Much of the current criticism of the administration of large organizations is basically a criticism of our failure to place the same emphasis on accountability that we do on authority and responsibility.
The one of the following acts which is MOST likely to insure accountability for the discharge of responsibilities inherent in the delegation of authority is the
    A. establishment of appropriate reports and controls
    B. organization of a methods analysis section
    C. delegation of authority so made as to support functional or homogeneous activities
    D. delegation of authority so made as to preserve unity of command
    E. decentralization of responsibility and authority

12. This statement has been made:
A man who is a top-notch executive in one organization would make a top-notch executive in any other organization, even if the organizations are as diverse as a sales agency and a research foundation.
This statement is, in general,
    A. *correct*; the characteristics required for a good executive are invariant with respect to organization
    B. *incorrect*; there is no way of predicting how a good executive in one organization would be in any other
    C. *correct*; while the characteristics required for a good executive vary from organization to organization, the common core requirements are great enough to insure similar performance
    D. *incorrect*; although some prediction can be made, different types of organizations require different types of executives
    E. *correct*; success as an executive does not depend upon "characteristics" but on the man; if he is able to direct and execute in one organization he will be able to do so in any other

13. Reported information is not needed at levels higher than those at which decisions are made on the basis of the information reported.
This statement is, in general,
    A. *correct*; if no action is to be taken on the basis of the information, the information is unnecessary
    B. *incorrect*; all information is of importance in arriving at a sound decision

C. *correct*; levels below the one at which the decision is made have need of the information
D. *incorrect*; levels below the one at which the decision is made do not have need of the information
E. *correct*; decisions should be made on the basis of information reported

14. Of the following, the characteristic of an organization which BEST shows that the organizational hierarchy is effective is that
    A. the department head commands the respect of the employees
    B. the organization is sufficiently flexible to assume functions in fields not related to his major field of endeavor
    C. responsibility has been appropriately delegated throughout the organization
    D. the department continues to function effectively even though there is continual turnover in the higher supervisory ranks
    E. no employee in the organization is subject to orders from more than one source

14.____

15. It is only because the primary purpose of traditional discipline has been to preserve the structure of command that a need has arisen for ameliorative safeguards such as a formal statement of "cause," right of hearing, and right of appeal.
    The BEST current practice with respect to discipline is that
    A. few ameliorative safeguards of the kind enumerated are desirable as their presence hurts the public service
    B. discipline is a means of controlling deviations from established authority
    C. the safeguards enumerated are not sufficient for the protection of the employee
    D. discipline should be based upon education, persuasion, and consultation
    E. unquestioned obedience to each order should not be expected but that a supervisor should be prepared at all times to demonstrate the reasonableness of his requests

15.____

16. Of the following types of work, the one for which a manual process is MOST usually to be preferred over a mechanized process is one in which the transactions are very
    A. numerous   B. similar   C. dissimilar
    D. predictable   E. unpredictable

16.____

17. Work flow charts are used in an organization PRIMARILY because they
    A. indicate present and future objectives clearly
    B. are frequently used records
    C. clearly indicate when each operation will be performed
    D. summarize the work procedures of the organization
    E. tend to clarify thinking by presenting certain facts clearly

17.____

5 (#3)

18. With respect to a report prepared by an IBM installation, the one of the following changes which is LEAST likely to cause a change in the procedure for preparing the report is a change in the
    A. volume of work
    B. source documents
    C. final report
    D. employees assigned
    E. time allowed for the preparation of the report

18.____

19. The one of the following which is NOT necessarily a characteristic of a good buying procedure is that it
    A. provides for proper analysis of purchases made
    B. is simple
    C. makes provision for substitutions where possible and necessary
    D. makes sealed bids mandatory
    E. recruits many bidders

19.____

20. Data relating to the operation of any unit should be accumulated and periodically summarized and analyzed PRIMARILY in order to
    A. point out the most efficient and least efficient workers
    B. determine the relative value of each procedure
    C. locate the elements of an operation which are unusually efficient or inefficient
    D. evaluate the importance of maintaining operating records and quotas
    E. compare the work performed by comparable units

20.____

21. Of the following, the MAJOR function of an administrative planning and research staff units is to
    A. investigate trouble points in the organization
    B. reorganize inefficient units
    C. assist the executive to plan future operations
    D. conduct continuous investigations and planning
    E. write the necessary operation and procedure manuals

21.____

22. The one of the following which does NOT require definition when setting up a work measurement system is the
    A. level of work accomplishment at which to measure
    B. work unit in which to measure
    C. time unit by which to measure
    D. acceptable quota for each activity
    E. reporting system to be used

22.____

23. During a discussion of the time unit that would be appropriate to measure employee-time in a work measurement program in a public agency, the man-day was suggested.
    This unit is
    A. *satisfactory*; record keeping will be kept to a minimum
    B. *unsatisfactory*; it will be difficult to verify the unit against official time records

23.____

C. *satisfactory*; it will be easy to verify the unit against official time records
D. *unsatisfactory*; its use will unnecessarily complicate record keeping
E. *satisfactory*; it permits more meaningful comparisons to be made between equal periods of time

24. As part of a space layout survey, an administrator instructed his subordinates to study the flow of work and sequence of operating procedures.
His MAJOR purposes in doing this was to determine
    A. the physical distribution and movement of personnel, material, and equipment
    B. the amount of space which is available and the amount of space which will be required
    C. the order in which the component steps in the different procedures are performed
    D. what future requirements will be, based on observable present trend
    E. how the distribution of personnel to various organization units is related to their space requirements

25. Before discussing a proposed office layout, the administrative officer stated, *"We intend to have a minimum number of private offices. We will assign private offices only where quiet is deemed essential or confidential conferences are required."*
The one of the following which is usually the MOST valid reason for this rule is that it
    A. permits proper placing of employees who deal with the public
    B. makes it easier to locate supervisors near the units they control
    C. tends to ensure that the work of each unit will flow continually forward within itself
    D. allows placing complementary units close together
    E. makes clerical supervision easier

KEY (CORRECT ANSWERS)

1.	D	11.	A
2.	C	12.	D
3.	E	13.	A
4.	A	14.	C
5.	C	15.	D
6.	E	16.	C
7.	D	17.	E
8.	D	18.	D
9.	E	19.	D
10.	A	20.	C

21. D
22. D
23. D
24. A
25. E

EXAMINATION SECTION
TEST 1

DIRECTIONS: Each question or incomplete statement is followed by several suggested answers or completions. Select the one that BEST answers the question or completes the statement. *PRINT THE LETTER OF THE CORRECT ANSWER IN THE SPACE AT THE RIGHT.*

1. Files are used to store

    A. data
    B. programs
    C. operating systems
    D. source programs
    E. all of the above

    1.____

2. MOST hard disks hold _____ bytes.

    A. 1-100 trillion
    B. 1-100 billion
    C. 1-100 million
    D. 1-1000
    E. less than 1000

    2.____

3. MOST floppy disks can store _____ bytes.

    A. 1-100 trillion
    B. 1-100 billion
    C. 1-100 million
    D. 1-1 million
    E. less than 1000

    3.____

4. A master file stores

    A. data about particular events
    B. relatively permanent data
    C. source copies of programs
    D. copies of other files
    E. data extracted from another file and held for a short term

    4.____

5. A transaction file stores

    A. data about particular events
    B. relatively permanent data
    C. source copies of programs
    D. copies of other files
    E. data extracted from another file and held for a short term

    5.____

6. A program file stores

    A. data about particular events
    B. relatively permanent data
    C. source copies of programs
    D. copies of other files
    E. data extracted from another file and held for a short term

    6.____

7. A backup file stores

    A. data about particular events
    B. relatively permanent data
    C. source copies of programs
    D. copies of other files
    E. data extracted from another file and held for a short term

    7.____

2 (#1)

8. Which of the following is NOT a type of storage method?   8.__

    A. EBCDIC   B. Packed hexadecimal
    C. Packed decimal   D. True binary
    E. ASCII

9. Which of the following is the storage method commonly used by IBM?   9.__

    A. EBCDIC   B. Packed hexadecimal
    C. Packed decimal   D. True binary
    E. ASCII

10. Which of the following is a very efficient numerical storage method?   10.__

    A. EBCDIC   B. Packed hexadecimal
    C. Packed decimal   D. True binary
    E. ASCII

11. Which of the following is the type of storage method commonly found on home or personal computers, as well as many mini-computers?   11.__

    A. EBCDIC   B. Packed hexadecimal
    C. Packed decimal   D. True binary
    E. ASCII

12. In the EBCDIC storage method,   12.__

    A. numbers follow letters
    B. letters follow numbers
    C. numbers are intermixed with letters
    D. numbers cannot be stored
    E. letters cannot be stored

13. In the ASCII storage method,   13.__

    A. numbers follow letters
    B. letters follow numbers
    C. numbers are intermixed with letters
    D. numbers cannot be stored
    E. letters cannot be stored

14. The collating sequence refers to   14.__

    A. the order of the letters in the alphabet
    B. the order of the digits 0 through 9
    C. the order of manufacturers of computers
    D. the order of numbers and letters relative to each other
    E. none of the above

15. A two-letter state abbreviation takes how many bytes of computer memory when stored in ASCII?   15.__

    A. 0   B. 1   C. 2
    D. 5   E. None of the above

16. A two-letter state abbreviation takes how many bytes of computer memory when stored in EBCDIC? 16._____

   A. 0 B. 1 C. 2
   D. 5 E. None of the above

17. An alternative to storing numeric data in EBCDIC is to store it in 17._____

   A. ZIP format B. true trinary C. true hexabinary
   D. true binary E. all of the above

18. Packed decimal means each decimal digit is stored in 18._____

   A. one nibble B. one byte C. ASCII format
   D. EBCDIC format E. all of the above

19. Generally speaking, alphanumeric data should be stored in 19._____

   A. nibbles B. straight binary C. EBCDIC
   D. packed decimal E. all of the above

20. Which statement below BEST describes a capability associated with virtual storage? 20._____

   A. It is possible to program as if more core is available than exists in the system
   B. All computers are now automatically compatible
   C. Only tapes and disks can be used for storage
   D. The programmer can write efficient programs while completely ignoring the nature of the computer system being used
   E. None of the above

KEY (CORRECT ANSWERS)

1. A   11. E
2. C   12. A
3. D   13. B
4. B   14. D
5. A   15. C

6. C   16. C
7. D   17. D
8. B   18. A
9. A   19. C
10. D   20. A

TEST 2

DIRECTIONS: Each question or incomplete statement is followed by several suggested answers or completions. Select the one that BEST answers the question or completes the statement. *PRINT THE LETTER OF THE CORRECT ANSWER IN THE SPACE AT THE RIGHT.*

1. Which of the following is NOT a common tape density?

    A. 800   B. 1600   C. 2400   D. 6250
    E. All are common densities

2. Which of the following is a common tape length?

    A. 800   B. 1600   C. 2400   D. 6250
    E. All are common densities

3. Blocking refers to the

    A. number of physical records in a logical record
    B. number of bytes in a record
    C. number of bytes per inch of tape
    D. number of logical records in a physical record
    E. the space between physical records

4. The inter block gap refers to the

    A. number of physical records in a logical record
    B. number of bytes in a record
    C. number of bytes per inch of tape
    D. number of logical records in a physical record
    E. the space between physical records

5. Density refers to the

    A. number of physical records in a logical record
    B. number of bytes in a record
    C. number of bytes per inch of tape
    D. number of logical records in a physical record
    E. the space between physical records

6. The record length refers to the

    A. number of physical records in a logical record
    B. number of bytes in a record
    C. number of bytes per inch of tape
    D. number of logical records in a physical record
    E. the space between physical records

7. Disks are BEST used in situations where

    A. we need to store ineexpensively
    B. we need to store historical data
    C. we want to process data sequentially
    D. we need to store data for on-line applications
    E. All of the above

8. Tape is BEST used in situations where 8.____

   A. we need to store data inexpensively
   B. we need to store historical data
   C. we want to process data sequentially
   D. we do not need to store data for on-line applications
   E. All of the above

9. Which of the following is NOT a direct access method? 9.____

   A. VSAM
   B. Sequential
   C. KSAM
   D. ISAM
   E. All of the above are direct access methods

10. A basing algorithm calculates a records location in a file using a(n) 10.____

    A. record address
    B. social security number
    C. key field like a social security number
    D. using the binary search strategy
    E. all of the above

11. The soundex algorithm converts 11.____

    A. numeric keys to disk addresses
    B. disk addresses to numeric keys
    C. disk addresses to alphanumeric keys
    D. alphanumeric keys to disk addresses
    E. disk addresses to collisions

12. A collision occurs if two records have the 12.____

    A. same record key
    B. hash to the same disk address
    C. same length
    D. same blocking factor
    E. same density

13. In designing a tape file, an analyst should consider which of the following factors? 13.____

    A. Record fields
    B. Sequential order of records
    C. Estimate the number of records in the file
    D. Calculate the record length
    E. All of the above

14. In designing a tape file, an analyst should consider which of the following factors? 14.___

    A. Order of fields in a record
    B. Placement of fields in a record
    C. An expansion area for future use
    D. Data storage method, EBCDIC or packed decimal
    E. All of the above

15. A record count tallies the number of 15.___

    A. records in the file
    B. number of fields in each record
    C. number of bytes in a record
    D. files in the database
    E. All of the above

16. The term backup means 16.___

    A. copying each record to a new record
    B. copying a file to tape
    C. copying a disk to memory
    D. deleting a file from disk
    E. deleting a file from a tape

17. The interblock gap is typically _____ inch(es). 17.___

    A. .05   B. .005   C. .5   D. 5   E. 50

18. In writing the schema, the analyst defines 18.___

    A. data sets
    B. data elements
    C. data type, numeric or alphanumeric
    D. slave data sets
    E. All of the above

19. Which of the following is a typical data manipulation language command? 19.___

    A. QUERY   B. LOCK   C. DML
    D. DDL   E. None of the above

20. Which of the following statements concerning index files and backup programs is TRUE? 20.___

    A. Index files may not be backed up.
    B. All appropriate index files are automatically backed up whenever a database file backup is created.
    C. Index files are often not backed up because they are so easily rebuilt.
    D. Index files must be backed up whenever their database files are backed up.
    E. None of the above

KEY (CORRECT ANSWERS)

1.	B	11.	D
2.	C	12.	B
3.	D	13.	E
4.	E	14.	E
5.	C	15.	A
6.	B	16.	B
7.	D	17.	C
8.	E	18.	E
9.	B	19.	B
10.	C	20.	C

EXAMINATION SECTION
TEST 1

DIRECTIONS: Each question or incomplete statement is followed by several suggested answers or completions. Select the one that BEST answers the question or completes the statement. *PRINT THE LETTER OF THE CORRECT ANSWER IN THE SPACE AT THE RIGHT.*

1. Each of the following is a measure that is likely to be included in the usability assessment of an online catalog, EXCEPT

    A. direct observations of search behavior
    B. focus groups
    C. benchmark comparisons
    D. transaction logs

    1.____

2. "Reformatting" electronic records means that

    A. they are moved from a proprietary legacy system that lacks software functionality to an open system
    B. they have been transferred from old storage media to new storage media with the same format specifications and without any loss in structure, content, or context
    C. records are exported or imported from one software environment to another without the loss of structure, content, or context even though the underlying bit stream has likely been altered
    D. there is a change to the underlying bit stream, but there is no change in the representation or intellectual content of the records

    2.____

3. An accession record typically includes each of the following, EXCEPT

    A. a brief bibliographic identification
    B. the MARC record
    C. the price paid for the item
    D. the accession number

    3.____

4. What is the term for the ability to move from citations in an article to those articles, and from articles to citations in a database?

    A. Click-wrap
    B. Bi-directional linking
    C. Bundling
    D. Hypertext

    4.____

5. A cross-reference that would be used to direct a user from a term that is not used to a term that is used is a

    A. *see* reference
    B. *see also* reference
    C. *NOT* reference
    D. *BT* reference

    5.____

6. Which of the following is a key legal issue of the Information Age?

    A. The digital divide
    B. Spam
    C. Underfunded infrastructure
    D. Copyright and fair use

7. Which of the following expenses is MOST likely to be included in a library's capital improvement budget?

    A. Library materials
    B. Salaries and wages
    C. Facilities maintenance
    D. Initial book stock

8. The archival longevity of CDs, DVDs, and videodiscs ranges from _____ years.

    A. 1-10
    B. 5-50
    C. 10-100
    D. 200-800

9. Which of the following is NOT a Web-based source of free electronic journals?

    A. Electronic Collections Online (ECO)
    B. University of Waterloo Electronic Library
    C. CIC Electronic Journals Collection
    D. New Jour archive

10. In the Dublin Core Metadata Initiative, an international effort to develop standard mechanisms for searching online resources, the _____ metadata element refers to the physical or digital manifestation of a resource.

    A. Format
    B. Type
    C. Identifier
    D. Description

11. Each of the following is typically used to increase precision in online searching, EXCEPT

    A. an "AND" operator
    B. truncation
    C. using additional concepts
    D. restricting by field

12. In _____ indexing, a human indexer or computer extracts from the title and/or text of a document one or more words or phrases to represent subject(s) of the work, for use as headings under which entries are made.

    A. post-coordinate
    B. string
    C. derivative
    D. assignment

13. A user seeking articles about archeology should be directed to Wilson's _____ Index.   13.____

    A. Social Sciences
    B. General Science
    C. Applied Science and Technology
    D. Humanities

14. Which of the following is NOT an example of a metapublisher?   14.____

    A. High Wire
    B. MetaPress
    C. Ingenta
    D. Northern Lights

15. A "network computer" is most accurately described as a(n)   15.____

    A. computer that access and gains all of its power from a network
    B. computer that operates a network
    C. computer that can access a network
    D. network that has the functional characteristics of a computer

16. Which of the following items is MOST likely to be excluded from materials budget at a large library?   16.____

    A. Media
    B. Serials
    C. Books
    D. Electronic resources

17. Issue number 8 of a journal is identified in the MLA citation format as   17.____

    A. (8)
    B. .8
    C. No. 8
    D. :8

18. In the MARC record, which of the following fields is LEAST likely to contain an access point?   18.____

    A. 0XX
    B. 1XX
    C. 4XX
    D. 7XX

19. The user of a thesaurus of indexing terms wants to get an idea of the number of entries a search for the term is likely to retrieve. Usually, the _____ note added to the entry will provide this.   19.____

    A. scope
    B. domain
    C. postings
    D. scatter

20. William Langer's *Encyclopedia of World History* is an example of _____ arrangement.

    A. weighted
    B. topical
    C. alphabetical
    D. chronological

21. Which of the following is an example of a highly developed string-indexing system?

    A. PRECIS
    B. WordSmith
    C. MARC
    D. CiteSeer

22. In digital libraries, the methods for achieving interoperability that continue to be used most widely are ones that have moderate functionality and a low cost. Each of the following is an example, EXCEPT

    A. Z39.50
    B. HTTP
    C. URL
    D. HTML

23. In the 2001 *New York Times Co. v. Tasini* decision, the Supreme Court ruled that

    A. publishers of newspapers and periodicals infringed on the copyrights of freelance writers by making the full text of their articles publicly available in computer databases without permission
    B. Congress's passage of the Copyright Term Extension Act, which extended the duration of copyrights from life of the author plus 50 years to the life of the author plus 70 years could be applied to copyrights that existed before the law was passed
    C. the effect of the use of a copyrighted work upon the potential market for or value of the copyrighted work would be a factor that would help define whether the use is "fair" under copyright law
    D. all works for which the statutory copyright period has expires are in the public domain

24. Examples of databases include
    I. Internet search engines
    II. online library catalogs
    III. electronic periodical indexes
    IV. FirstSearch

    A. I and II
    B. II only
    C. II, III and IV
    D. I, II, III and IV

25. A major descriptor in the index entry of a bibliographic record is usually indicated by   25.____

    A. underlining
    B. italics
    C. an asterisk (*)
    D. ALL CAPS

KEY (CORRECT ANSWERS)

1. D	6. D	11. B	16. D	21. A
2. D	7. D	12. C	17. B	22. A
3. B	8. C	13. D	18. A	23. A
4. B	9. A	14. D	19. C	24. D
5. A	10. A	15. A	20. D	25. C

TEST 2

DIRECTIONS: Each question or incomplete statement is followed by several suggested answers or completions. Select the one that BEST answers the question or completes the statement. *PRINT THE LETTER OF THE CORRECT ANSWER IN THE SPACE AT THE RIGHT.*

1. A preservation administrator at a library plans to use digital imaging technology to create a digital document archive. Typically, which of the following steps in this process is performed FIRST?

    A. Image enhancement
    B. Bibliographic control
    C. Intellectual control
    D. Conversion

    1.___

2. When added to HTML code, cascading style sheets

    A. allow Web site developers to automatically apply the same layout to multiple documents
    B. match source citations with target resources
    C. force a text message to pop up and replace the information content of an on-screen image
    D. allow for the running of multiple small programs within the Web-page interface

    2.___

3. A user types in the term "lights" into the field of a search engine, and the results include not only "lights" but "light," "lighting," "lit," and others. The search engine offers the feature known as

    A. limits
    B. truncation
    C. stemming
    D. stop words

    3.___

4. After a single copy of a one-volume work, has been acquired and processed by the library, the _____ record is attached to the full bibliographic record to track the copy.

    A. item
    B. order
    C. holdings
    D. check-in

    4.___

5. Technical metadata that describe the physical characteristics of a resource are a subcategory of _____ metadata.

    A. structural
    B. digital
    C. administrative
    D. descriptive

    5.___

6. A librarian is attempting to determine whether the online version of a journal is equivalent to its print counterpart. The librarian should check to see that both versions include

    I. the complete text of articles, not merely an abstract or summary
    II. letters to the editor, book reviews, feature columns, and advertisements
    III. illustrations and graphics
    IV. cross-references

    A. I and II
    B. I, II and III
    C. III and IV
    D. I, II, III and IV

6._____

7. The optimal temperature for the storage of magnetic media is around _____ degrees F.

    A. 45
    B. 55
    C. 65
    D. 75

7._____

8. The abbreviation "TOP" on a publisher's invoice usually means

    A. the requested item is nonreturnable
    B. cash is required with the order
    C. there is a new edition of the item pending
    D. the requested item is out of print for the time being

8._____

9. Pricing for a site license granted by a software vendor to a library is LEAST likely to be priced according to the

    A. terms regarding sharing and use of copies
    B. number of users in the community
    C. potential number of uses of specific content
    D. number of simultaneous users

9._____

10. Which of the following is a periodical that prints feature articles on applications of computer technologies in libraries and reviews of technology products, and which maintains a very practical focus?

    A. *Information Outlook*
    B. *Library Hi-Tech*
    C. *Computers in Libraries*
    D. *Webopedia*

10._____

11. Which of the following is a disadvantage associated with library system automation?

    A. More limited options for searching for information
    B. Increased likelihood of discouraging patrons from using the catalog
    C. Creation of additional tasks and skill sets for staff
    D. Greater difficulty in inventories and holding counts

11._____

12. Which of the following is a service that provides the online full-text of literary works in the public domain?   12.____

    A. EBSCO
    B. Northern Lights
    C. JSTOR
    D. Project Gutenberg

13. In digital libraries, many of the most recent developments in achieving interoperability are attempts to add substantial functionality at a moderate cost. Which of the following is NOT an example of this approach?   13.____

    A. XML
    B. SGML
    C. Unicode
    D. The Dublin Core

14. *http://www.lcweb.loc.gov/acq/conser/module12.html*   14.____
    In the above URL, *acq/conser* designates a

    A. filename
    B. server or hostname
    C. protocol or access scheme
    D. directory or path

15. In the Library of Congress Classification System, indexes are cataloged under   15.____

    A. LI
    B. AS
    C. IN
    D. AI

16. Which of the following periodical indexes does NOT offer full-text articles?   16.____

    A. *InfoTrac*
    B. *Readers' Guide to Periodical Literature,*
    C. *EBSCOhost*
    D. *ProQuest*

17. A scholarly journal is LEAST likely to be published   17.____

    A. weekly
    B. monthly
    C. quarterly
    D. semiannually

18. In the MLA style, items in a bibliography are arranged according to   18.____

    A. the author's surname
    B. *Library of Congress Subject Headings* classification
    C. importance
    D. title

19. A library is in the process of determining the extent of its resources. Which of the following would be identified as an "input" measure?

    A. Ratio of circulation
    B. Interlibrary loan/document delivery lending turnaround time, fill rate, and unit cost
    C. Percent of total library budget expended
    D. Number of reference questions answered

20. Which of the following MARC fields is variable in length?

    A. 001
    B. 003
    C. 005
    D. 007

21. Which of the following online databases is produced by a database vendor, rather than a subscription agent?

    A. EBSCO
    B. OCLC's Electronic Collections Online (ECO)
    C. Rowe-Com's Information Quest
    D. Blackwell Electronic Journal Navigator (EJN)

22. In a classification schedule, a _____ note instructs the cataloger to classify works in multiple locations.

    A. scope
    B. gather
    C. scatter
    D. distribution

23. Approximately what percentage of MARC fields are widely used throughout most bibliographic records?

    A. 10
    B. 30
    C. 60
    D. 90

24. The client/server model of computing, of which the Internet is the most conspicuous example, is characterized by
    I. each node or workstation having equivalent responsibilities
    II. server computers running special software that organizes and manages information
    III. individuals using client computers to access information
    IV. server computers containing the information that is accessed by users

    A. I and II
    B. I, II, and III
    C. II, III and IV
    D. I, II, III and IV

25. In most libraries, periodical issues are bound together when the issues have 25.___
    A. preserved on microform
    B. been analyzed by an indexing service
    C. fill a single shelf
    D. formed a complete volume

KEY (CORRECT ANSWERS)

1. D	6. B	11. C	16. B	21. B
2. A	7. C	12. D	17. A	22. C
3. C	8. D	13. B	18. A	23. A
4. A	9. A	14. D	19. C	24. C
5. C	10. C	15. D	20. B	25. D

DOCUMENTS AND FORMS
PREPARING WRITTEN MATERIALS
EXAMINATION SECTION
TEST 1

DIRECTIONS: Each question or incomplete statement is followed by several suggested answers or completions. Select the one that BEST answers the question or completes the statement. *PRINT THE LETTER OF THE CORRECT ANSWER IN THE SPACE AT THE RIGHT.*

1. The office layout chart is a sketch of the physical arrangement of the office to which has been added the flow lines of the principal work performed there.
   Which one of the following states the BEST advantage of superimposing the work flow onto the desk layout?

   A. Lighting and acoustics can be improved.
   B. Line and staff relationships can be determined.
   C. Obvious misarrangements can be corrected.
   D. The number of delays can be determined.

   1._____

2. An advantage of the multiple process chart over the flow process chart is that the multiple process chart shows the

   A. individual worker's activity
   B. number of delays
   C. sequence of operations
   D. simultaneous flow of work in several departments

   2._____

3. Of the following, which is the MAJOR advantage of a microfilm record retention system?

   A. Filing can follow the terminal digit system.
   B. Retrieving documents from the files is faster.
   C. Significant space is saved in storing records.
   D. To read a microfilm record, a film reader is not necessary.

   3._____

4. Assume that you are in the process of eliminating unnecessary forms.
   The answer to which one of the following questions would be LEAST relevant?

   A. Could the information be obtained elsewhere?
   B. Is the form properly designed?
   C. Is the form used as intended?
   D. Is the purpose of the form essential to the operation?

   4._____

5. Use of color in forms adds to their cost. Sometimes, however, the use of color will greatly simplify procedure and more than pay for itself in time saved and errors eliminated.
   This is ESPECIALLY true when

   A. a form passes through many reviewers
   B. considerable sorting is required
   C. the form is other than a standard size
   D. the form will not be sent through the mail

   5._____

6. Of the following techniques, the one *generally* employed and considered BEST in forms design is to provide writing lines into boxes with captions printed in small type
   A. centered in the lower part of the box
   B. centered in the upper part of the box
   C. in the upper left-hand corner of the box
   D. in the lower right-hand corner of the box

7. Many forms authorities advocate the construction of a functional forms file or index. If such a file is set up, the MOST effective way of classifying forms for such an index is classification by
   A. department
   B. form number
   C. name or type of form
   D. subject to which the form applies

8. Of the following, the symbol as used in a systems flow chart denotes
   A. decision
   B. document
   C. manual operation
   D. process

9. Assume you are assigned to analyze the details of the procedures a clerk follows in order to complete filling out an invoice or a requisition. Your purpose is to simplify and shorten the procedure he has been trained to use.
   The BEST appropriate chart for this purpose would be the
   A. block flow diagram   B. flow process chart
   C. forms flow chart   D. work distribution chart

10. What *generally* is the PRINCIPAL objection to the use of form letters? The
    A. difficulty of developing a form letter to serve the purpose
    B. excessive time involved in selecting the proper form letter
    C. errors in selecting form letters
    D. impersonality of form letters

11. In process charting, the symbol which is used when conditions (except those which intentionally change the physical or chemical characteristics of the object) do not permit or require immediate performance, is

12. Assume that you are making a study of a central headquarters office which processes   12.____
claims received from a number of district offices. You notice the following problems:
Some employees are usually busy, while others doing the same kind of work in the same
grade have little to do; high level professional people frequently spend considerable time
searching for files in the file room. Which of the following charts would be MOST useful to
record and analyze the data needed to help solve these problems?

    A. Forms distribution chart
    B. Process chart
    C. Space layout chart
    D. Work distribution chart

13. Which of the following questions has the LEAST significant bearing on the analysis of the   13.____
paperwork flow?

    A. How is the work brought into the department and how is it taken away?
    B. How many work stations are involved in processing the work within the department?
    C. Is the work received and removed in the proper quantity?
    D. Where is the supervisor's desk located in relationship to those he supervises?

14. Which of the following does NOT have significant bearing on the arrangement,   14.____
sequence, and zoning of information into box captions? The

    A. layout of the source documents from which the information is taken
    B. logical flow of data
    C. needs of forms to be prepared from this form
    D. type of print to be employed

15. In determining the space requirements of a form and the size of the boxes to be used,   15.____
PRIMARY consideration should be given to the

    A. distribution of the form
    B. method of entry, i.e., handwritten or machine, and type of machine
    C. number of copies
    D. number of items to be entered

16. Of the following, the BEST technique to follow when providing instructions for the completion and routing of a form is to   16.____

    A. imprint the instructions on the face of the form
    B. imprint the instructions on the back of the form
    C. provide a written procedure to accompany the form
    D. provide verbal instructions when issuing the form

17. A forms layout style where a separate space in the shape of a box is provided for each   17.____
item of information requested and the caption or question for each item is shown in the
upper left-hand corner of each box, is known as the

    A. box style
    B. check box style
    C. check list style
    D. check box and check list style

18. The BEST type of chart to use in showing the absolute movement or change of a continuous series of data over a period of time, such as changes in prices, employment or   18.____
expenses, is *usually* a

A. bar chart B. line chart
C. multiple bar chart D. pie chart

19. In order to secure information on several specific points from all the tenants of a project, it has been suggested that a questionnaire be distributed to be completed and returned by the tenants.
The use of such a procedure is, *generally*,

    A. *desirable*, because it is a valuable means of building the cooperative relationship which should exist between tenants and management
    B. *desirable*, because it provides a written record of each tenant's reply
    C. *undesirable*, because distribution and collection of questionnaires is time-consuming
    D. *undesirable*, because it makes no provision for the expression of related information or viewpoints

20. A functional forms file is a collection of forms which are grouped by

    A. purpose B. department C. title D. subject

21. All of the following are reasons to consult a records retention schedule EXCEPT one. Which one is that? To determine

    A. whether something should be filed
    B. how long something should stay in file
    C. who should be assigned to filing
    D. when something on file should be destroyed

22. Listed below are four of the steps in the process of preparing correspondence for filing. If they were to be put in logical sequence, the SECOND step would be

    A. preparing cross-reference sheets or cards
    B. coding the correspondence using a classification system
    C. sorting the correspondence in the order to be filed
    D. checking for follow-up action required and preparing a follow-up slip

23. New material added to a file folder should *usually* be inserted

    A. in the order of importance (the most important in front)
    B. in the order of importance (the most important in back)
    C. chronologically (most recent in front)
    D. chronologically (most recent in back)

24. An individual is looking for a name in the white pages of a telephone directory. Which of the following BEST describes the system of filing found there? A(n)

    A. alphabetic file B. sequential file
    C. locator file D. index file

25. The MAIN purpose of a tickler file is to

    A. help prevent overlooking matters that require future attention
    B. check on adequacy of past performance
    C. pinpoint responsibility for recurring daily tasks
    D. reduce the volume of material kept in general files

KEY (CORRECT ANSWERS)

1. C
2. D
3. C
4. B
5. B

6. C
7. D
8. A
9. B
10. D

11. C
12. D
13. D
14. D
15. B

16. A
17. A
18. B
19. B
20. A

21. C
22. A
23. C
24. A
25. A

TEST 2

1. A *good* record-keeping system includes all of the following procedures EXCEPT the

    A. filing of useless records
    B. destruction of certain files
    C. transferring of records from one type of file to another
    D. creation of inactive files

2. A new program is being set up for which certain new forms will be needed. You have been asked to design these forms.
   Of the following, the FIRST step you should take in planning the forms is

    A. finding out the exact purpose for which each form will be used
    B. deciding what size of paper should be used for each form
    C. determining whether multiple copies will be needed for any of the forms
    D. setting up a new filing system to handle the new forms

3. Assume that your department is being moved to new and larger quarters, and that you have been asked to suggest an office layout for the central clerical office.
   Of the following, your FIRST step in planning the new layout should *ordinarily* be to

    A. find out how much money has been budgeted for furniture and equipment
    B. make out *work-flow* and *traffic-flow* charts for the clerical operations
    C. measure each piece of furniture and equipment that is presently in use
    D. determine which files should be moved to a storage area or destroyed

4. In modern office layouts, screens and dividers are often used instead of walls to set off working groups. Advantages given for this approach have included *all* of the following EXCEPT

    A. more frequent communication between different working groups
    B. reduction in general noise level
    C. fewer objections from employees who are transferred to different groups
    D. cost savings from increased sharing of office equipment

5. Of the following, the CHIEF reason for moving less active material from active to inactive files is to

    A. dispose of material that no longer has any use
    B. keep the active files down to a manageable size
    C. make sure that no material over a year old remains in active files
    D. separate temporary records from permanent records

6. On a general organization chart, staff positions NORMALLY should be pictured

    A. directly above the line positions to which they report
    B. to the sides of the main flow lines
    C. within the box of the highest level subordinate positions pictured
    D. directly below the line positions which report to them

7. When an administrator is diagramming an office layout, of the following, his PRIMARY job, *generally,* should be to indicate the

   A. lighting intensities that will be required by each operation
   B. noise level that will be produced by the various equipment employed in the office
   C. direction of the work flow and the distance involved in each transfer
   D. durability of major pieces of office equipment currently in use or to be utilized

8. One common guideline or rule-of-thumb ratio for evaluating the efficiency of files is the number of records requested divided by the number of records filed.
   Generally, if this ratio is very low, it would point MOST directly to the need for

   A. improving the indexing and coding system
   B. improving the charge-out procedures
   C. exploring the need for transferring records from active storage to the archives
   D. exploring the need to encourage employees to keep more records in their private files

9. The GREATEST percentage of money spent on preparing and keeping the usual records in an office, *generally,* is expended for which one of the following?

   A. Renting space in which to place the record-keeping equipment
   B. Paying salaries of record-preparing and record-keeping personnel
   C. Depreciation of purchased record-preparation and record-keeping equipment
   D. Paper and forms upon which to place the records

10. The MAXIMUM number of 2 3/4" x 4 1/4" size forms which may be obtained from two reams of 17" x 22" paper is

    A. 4,000   B. 8,000   C. 16,000   D. 32,000

11. Word processing computer applications (i.e. Microsoft Word) generally provide all of the following advantages as compared to electric word processors EXCEPT

    A. documents save to disk automatically
    B. ability to include customized graphs and charts in a document
    C. wider selection of available fonts
    D. easily customized page orientation

12. Generally, the actual floor space occupied by a standard letter-size office file cabinet, when closed, is, *most nearly,*

    A. 1/2 square foot   B. 3 square feet
    C. 7 square feet   D. 11 square feet

13. In general, the CHIEF economy of using multicopy forms is in

    A. the paper on which the form is printed
    B. printing the form
    C. employee time
    D. carbon paper

14. Suppose your supervisor has asked you to develop a form to record certain information needed. The FIRST thing you should do is to

    A. determine the type of data that will be recorded repeatedly, so that it can be pre-printed
    B. study the relationship of the form to the job to be accomplished, so that the form can be planned
    C. determine the information that will be recorded in the same place on each copy of the form, so that it can be used as a check
    D. find out who will be responsible for supplying the information so that space can be provided for their signatures

15. Of the following, which is usually the MOST important guideline in writing business letters? A letter should be

    A. neat
    B. written in a formalized style
    C. written in clear language intelligible to the reader
    D. written in the past tense

16. Suppose you are asked to edit a policy statement. You note that personal pronouns like *you*, *we*, and *I* are used freely.
    Which of the following statements BEST applies to this use of personal pronouns? It

    A. is proper usage because written business language should not be different from carefully spoken business language
    B. requires correction because it is ungrammatical
    C. is proper because it is clearer and has a warmer tone
    D. requires correction because policies should be expressed in an impersonal manner

17. Good business letters are coherent. To be *coherent* means to

    A. keep only one unifying idea in the message
    B. present the total message
    C. use simple, direct words for the message
    D. tie together the various ideas in the message

18. Proper division of a letter into paragraphs requires that the writer of business letters should, as much as possible, be sure that

    A. each paragraph is short
    B. each paragraph develops discussion of just one topic
    C. each paragraph repeats the theme of the total message
    D. there are at least two paragraphs for every message

19. An editor is given a letter with this initial paragraph *We have received your letter, which we read with interest, and we are happy to respond to your question. In fact, we talked with several people in our office to get ideas to send to you.*
    Which of the following is it MOST reasonable for the editor to conclude? The paragraph is

    A. concise   B. communicating something of value
    C. unnecessary   D. coherent

20. Suppose that one of your duties is to dictate responses to routine requests from the pub- 20._____
lic for information. A letter writer asks for information which, as expressed in a one-sen-
tence, explicit agency rule, cannot be given out to the public.
Of the following ways of answering the letter, which is the MOST efficient?

   A. Quote verbatim that section of the agency rules which prohibits giving this information to the public
   B. Without quoting the rule, explain why you cannot accede to the request and suggest alternative sources
   C. Describe how carefully the request was considered before classifying it as subject
to the rule forbidding the issuance of such information
   D. Acknowledge receipt of the letter and advise that the requested information is not
released to the public

21. Suppose you have been asked to write and to prepare for reproduction new departmen- 21._____
tal vacation leave regulations. After you have written the new regulations, all of which fit
on one page, which one of the following would be the BEST method of reproducing 800
copies?

   A. An outside private printer, because you can best maintain confidentiality using this
technique
   B. Using your own computer's printer/copier, because it is most convenient
   C. Giving the job to a coworker in another department who does this type of work
more frequently, since the coworker is more familiar with the process
   D. Using a high-volume color copier, because it is fastest and of highest quality

22. The files in your office have been overcrowded and difficult to work with since you started 22._____
working there. One day your supervisor is transferred and another assistant in your office
decides to discard three drawers of the oldest materials.
For him to take this action is

   A. *desirable;* it will facilitate handling the more active materials
   B. *desirable;* no file should be removed from its point of origin
   C. *desirable;* there is no need to burden a new supervisor with unnecessary informa-
tion
   D. *undesirable;* no file should be discarded without first noting what material has been
discarded

23. You have been criticized by the general supervisor because of spelling errors in some of 23._____
your typing. You have only copied the reports as written and you realize that the errors
occurred in work given to you by your immediate supervisor.
Of the following, the BEST way for you to handle this situation is to

   A. tell the general supervisor that the spelling errors are your immediate supervisor's,
not yours, because they occur only when you type his reports
   B. tell the general supervisor that you only type the reports as given to you, without
indicating anyone
   C. inform your immediate supervisor that you have been unjustly criticized because of
his spelling errors and politely request that he be more careful in the future
   D. use a dictionary whenever you have doubt regarding spelling

24. You have recently found several items misfiled. You believe that this occurred because a new assistant in your section has been making mistakes.
    The BEST course of action for you to take is to

    A. refile the material and say nothing about it
    B. send your supervisor an anonymous note of complaint about the filing errors
    C. show the errors to the new assistant and tell him why they are errors in filing
    D. tell your supervisor that the new assistant makes a lot of errors in filing

24.____

KEY (CORRECT ANSWERS)

1. A
2. A
3. B
4. B
5. B

6. B
7. C
8. C
9. B
10. D

11. A
12. B
13. C
14. B
15. C

16. D
17. D
18. B
19. C
20. A

21. D
22. D
23. D
24. C

RECORD KEEPING
EXAMINATION SECTION
TEST 1

DIRECTIONS: Each question or incomplete statement is followed by several suggested answers or completions. Select the one that BEST answers the question or completes the statement. *PRINT THE LETTER OF THE CORRECT ANSWER IN THE SPACE AT THE RIGHT.*

Questions 1-15.

DIRECTIONS: Questions 1 through 15 are to be answered on the basis of the following list of company names below. Arrange a file alphabetically, word-by-word, disregarding punctuation, conjunctions, and apostrophes. Then answer the questions.

    A Bee C Reading Materials
    ABCO Parts
    A Better Course for Test Preparation
    AAA Auto Parts Co.
    A-Z Auto Parts, Inc.
    Aabar Books
    Abbey, Joanne
    Boman-Sylvan Law Firm
    BMW Autowerks
    C Q Service Company
    Chappell-Murray, Inc.
    E&E Life Insurance
    Emcrisco
    Gigi Arts
    Gordon, Jon & Associates
    SOS Plumbing
    Schmidt, J.B. Co.

1. Which of these files should appear FIRST?
   A. ABCO Parts
   B. A Bee C Reading Materials
   C. A Better Course for Test Preparation
   D. AAA Auto Parts Co.

2. Which of these files should appear SECOND?
   A. A-Z Auto Parts, Inc.
   B. A Bee C Reading Materials
   C. A Better Course for Test Preparation
   D. AAA Auto Parts Co.

3. Which of these files should appear THIRD?
   A. ABCO Parts
   B. A Bee C Reading Materials
   C. Aabar Books
   D. AAA Auto Parts Co.

   3._____

4. Which of these files should appear FOURTH?
   A. Aabar Books
   B. ABCO Parts
   C. Abbey, Joanne
   D. AAA Auto Parts Co.

   4._____

5. Which of these files should appear LAST?
   A. Gordon, Jon & Associates
   B. Gigi Arts
   C. Schmidt, J.B. Co.
   D. SOS Plumbing

   5._____

6. Which of these files should appear between A-Z Auto Parts, Inc. and Abbey, Joanne?
   A. A Bee C Reading Materials
   B. AAA Auto Parts Co.
   C. ABCO Parts
   D. A Better Course for Test Preparation

   6._____

7. Which of these files should appear between ABCO Parts and Aabar Books?
   A. A Bee C Reading Materials
   B. Abbey, Joanne
   C. Aabar Books
   D. A-Z Auto Parts

   7._____

8. Which of these files should appear between Abbey, Joanne and Boman-Sylvan Law Firm?
   A. A Better Course for Test Preparation
   B. BMW Autowerks
   C. Chappell-Murray, Inc.
   D. Aabar Books

   8._____

9. Which of these files should appear between Abbey, Joanne and C Q Service?
   A. A-Z Auto Parts, Inc.
   B. BMW Autowerks
   C. Choices A and B
   D. Chappell-Murray, Inc.

   9._____

10. Which of these files should appear between C Q Service Company and Emcrisco?
    A. Chappell-Murray, Inc.
    B. E&E Life Insurance
    C. Gigi Arts
    D. Choices A and B

    10._____

11. Which of these files should NOT appear between C Q Service Company and E&E Life Insurance?
    A. Gordon, Jon & Associates
    B. Emcrisco
    C. Gigi Arts
    D. All of the above

    11._____

12. Which of these files should appear between Chappell-Murray, Inc. and 12.____
    Gigi Arts?
    A. C Q Service Inc., E&E Life Insurance, and Emcrisco
    B. Emcrisco, E&E Life Insurance, and Gordon, Jon & Associates
    C. E&E Life Insurance, and Emcrisco
    D. Emcrisco and Gordon, Jon & Associates

13. Which of these files should appear between Gordon, Jon & Associates and 13.____
    SOS Plumbing?
    A. Gigi Arts   B. Schmidt, J.B. Co.
    C. Choices A and B   D. None of the above

14. Each of the choices lists the four files in their proper alphabetical order 14.____
    EXCEPT
    A. E&E Life Insurance; Gigi Arts; Gordon, Jon & Associates; SOS Plumbing
    B. E&E Life Insurance; Emcrisco; Gigi Arts; SOS Plumbing
    C. Emcrisco; Gordon, Jon & Associates; SOS Plumbing; Schmidt, J.B. Co.
    D. Emcrisco; Gigi Arts; Gordon, Jon & Associates; SOS Plumbing

15. Which of the choices lists the four files in their proper alphabetical order? 15.____
    A. Gigi Arts; Gordon, Jon & Associates; SOS Plumbing; Schmidt, J.B. Co.
    B. Gordon, Jon & Associates; Gigi Arts; Schmidt, J.B. Co.; SOS Plumbing
    C. Gordon, Jon & Associates; Gigi Arts; SOS Plumbing; Schmidt, J.B. Co.
    D. Gigi Arts; Gordon, Jon & Associates; Schmidt, J.B. Co.; SOS Plumbing

16. The alphabetical filing order of two businesses with identical names is 16.____
    determined by the
    A. length of time each business has been operating
    B. addresses of the businesses
    C. last name of the company president
    D. no one of the above

17. In an alphabetical filing system, if a business name includes a number, it should 17.____
    be
    A. disregarded
    B. considered a number and placed at the end of an alphabetical section
    C. treated as though it were written in words and alphabetized accordingly
    D. considered a number and placed at the beginning of an alphabetical
       section

18. If a business name includes a contraction (such as *don't* or *it's*), how should 18.____
    that word be treated in an alphabetical system?
    A. Divide the word into its separate parts and treat it as two words
    B. Ignore the letters that come after the apostrophe
    C. Ignore the word that contains the contraction
    D. Ignore the apostrophe and consider all letters in the contraction

19. In what order should the parts of an address be considered when using an alphabetical filing system?   19._____
    A. City or town; state; street name; house or building number
    B. State; city or town; street name; house or building number
    C. House or building number; street name; city or town; state
    D. Street name; city or town; state

20. A business record should be cross-referenced when a(n)   20._____
    A. organization is known by an abbreviated name
    B. business has a name change because of a sale, incorporation, or other reason
    C. business is known by a *coined* or common name which differs from a dictionary spelling
    D. all of the above

21. A geographical filing system is MOST effective when   21._____
    A. location is more important than name
    B. many names or titles sound alike
    C. dealing with companies who have offices all over the world
    D. filing personal and business files

Questions 22-25.

DIRECTIONS: Questions 22 through 25 are to be answered on the basis of the list of items below, which are to be filed geographically. Organize the items geographically and then answer the questions.

   I.   University Press at Berkeley, U.S.
   II. Maria Sanchez, Mexico City, Mexico
   III. Great Expectations Ltd. in London, England
   IV. Justice League, Cape Town, South Africa, Africa
   V.   Crown Pearls Ltd. in London, England
   VI. Joseph Prasad in London, England

22. Which of the following arrangements of the items is composed according to the policy of: *Continent, Country, City, Firm or Individual Name*?   22._____
    A. V, III, IV, VI, II, I   B. IV, V, III, VI, II, I
    C. I, IV, V, III, VI, II   D. IV, V, III, VI, I, II

23. Which of the following files is arranged according to the policy of: 23._____
    Continent, Country, City, Firm or Individual Name?
    A. South Africa; Africa; Cape Town; Justice League
    B. Mexico; Mexico City; Maria Sanchez
    C. North America; United States; Berkeley; University Press
    D. England; Europe; London; Prasad, Joseph

5 (#1)

24. Which of the following arrangements of the items is composed according to the policy of: *Country, City, Firm or Individual Name*?   24.____
    A. V, VI, III, II, IV, I
    B. I, V, VI, III, II, IV
    C. VI, V, III, II, IV, I
    D. V, III, VI, II, IV, I

25. Which of the following files is arranged according to a policy of: *Country, City, Firm or Individual Name*?   25.____
    A. England; London; Crown Pearls Ltd.
    B. North America; United States; Berkeley; University Press
    C. Africa; Cape Town; Justice League
    D. Mexico City; Mexico; Maria Sanchez

26. Under which of the following circumstances would a phonetic filing system be MOST effective?   26.____
    A. When the person in charge of filing can't spell very well
    B. With large files with names that sound alike
    C. With large files with names that are spelled alike
    D. All of the above

Questions 27-29.

DIRECTIONS: Questions 27 through 29 are to be answered on the basis of the following list of numerical files.

    I.   391-023-100
    II. 361-132-170
    III. 385-732-200
    IV. 381-432-150
    V.   391-632-387
    VI. 361-423-303
    VII. 391-123-271

27. Which of the following arrangements of the files follows a consecutive-digit system?   27.____
    A. II, III, IV, I   B. I, V, VII, III   C. II, IV, III, I   D. III, I, V, VII

28. Which of the following arrangements follows a terminal-digit system?   28.____
    A. I, VII, II, IV, III
    B. II, I, IV, V, VII
    C. VII, VI, V, IV, III
    D. I, IV, II, III, VII

29. Which of the following lists follows a middle-digit system?   29.____
    A. I, VII, II, VI, IV, V, III
    B. I, II, VII, IV, VI, V, III
    C. VII, II, I, III, V, VI, IV
    D. VII, I, II, IV, VI, V, III

Questions 30-31.

DIRECTIONS: Questions 30 and 31 are to be answered on the basis of the following information.

   I. Reconfirm Laura Bates appointment with James Caldecort on December 12 at 9:30 A.M.
   II. Laurence Kinder contact Julia Lucas on August 3 and set up a meeting for week of September 23 at 4 P.M.
   III. John Lutz contact Larry Waverly on August 3 and set up appointment for September 23 at 9:30 A.M.
   IV. Call for tickets for Gerry Stanton August 21 for New Jersey on September 23, flight 143 at 4:43 P.M.

30. A chronological file for the above information would be
    A. IV, III, II, I   B. III, II, IV, I   C. IV, II, III, I   D. III, I, II, IV

31. Using the above information, a chronological file for the date September 23 would be
    A. II, III, IV   B. III, I, IV   C. III, II, IV   D. IV, III, II

Questions 32-34.

DIRECTIONS: Questions 32 through 34 are to be answered on the basis of the following information.

   I. Call Roger Epstein, Ashoke Naipaul, Jon Anderson, and Sara Washingon on April 19 at 1:00 P.M. to set up meeting with Alika D'Ornay for June 6 in New York.
   II. Call Martin Ames before noon on April 19 to confirm afternoon meeting with Bob Greenwood on April 20th.
   III. Set up meeting room at noon for 2:30 P.M. meeting on April 19th.
   IV. Ashley Stanton contact Bob Greenwood at 9:00 A.M. on April 20 and set up meeting for June 6 at 8:30 A.M.
   V. Carol Guiland contact Shelby Van Ness during afternoon of April 20 and set up meeting for June 6 at 10:00 A.M.
   VI. Call airline and reserve tickets on June 6 for Roger Epstein trip to Denver on July 8.
   VII. Meeting at 2:30 P.M. on April 19th.

32. A chronological file for all of the above information would be
    A. II, I, III, VII, V, IV, VI   B. III, VII, II, I, IV, V, VI
    C. III, VII, I, II, V, IV, VI   D. II, III, I, VII, IV, V, VI

33. A chronological file for the date of April 19th would be
    A. II, III, VII, I   B. II, III, I, VII   C. VII, I, III, II   D. III, VII, I, II

34. Add the following information to the file, and then create a chronological file for April 20th: VIII. April 20: 3:00 P.M. meeting between Bob Greenwood and Martin Ames.
    A. IV, V, VIII   B. IV, VIII, V   C. VIII, V, IV   D. V, IV, VIII

34._____

35. The PRIMARY advantage of computer records over a manual system is
    A. speed of retrieval
    B. accuracy
    C. cost
    D. potential file loss

35._____

KEY (CORRECT ANSWERS)

1. B	11. D	21. A	31. C
2. C	12. C	22. B	32. D
3. D	13. B	23. C	33. B
4. A	14. C	24. D	34. A
5. D	15. D	25. A	35. A
6. C	16. B	26. B	
7. B	17. C	27. C	
8. B	18. D	28. D	
9. C	19. A	29. A	
10. D	20. D	30. B	

EXAMINATION SECTION
TEST 1

DIRECTIONS: Each question or incomplete statement is followed by several suggested answers or completions. Select the one that *BEST* answers the question or completes the statement. *PRINT THE LETTER OF THE CORRECT ANSWER IN THE SPACE AT THE RIGHT.*

1. The MOST important characteristic of a tickler card file is that the cards are arranged according to

    A. subject matter
    B. the date on which action is to be taken
    C. the name of the individual on the card
    D. the order of importance of the items contained on the cards

2. As a clerk in a city department, one of your duties is to maintain the files in your bureau. Material from these files is sometimes used by other bureaus. You frequently find that you are unable to locate some material because it has been removed from the files and is evidently being used by some other bureau. The BEST way to correct this situation is to

    A. have an out-of-file card filled out and filed when ever material is borrowed from the files
    B. forbid employees of other bureaus to borrow material from the files unless they promise to return it promptly
    C. provide other bureaus with duplicate files
    D. notify your supervisor whenever an employee from another bureau is slow in returning material to the files

3. A transfer file is used primarily to

    A. carry records from one office to another
    B. store inactive records
    C. hold records that are constantly used by more than one bureau of an organization
    D. hold confidential records

4. When a record is borrowed from the files, the file clerk puts a substitution or *out* card in its place. Of the following, the information that is LEAST commonly placed on the *out* card is

    A. who borrowed the record
    B. when the record was borrowed
    C. why the record was borrowed
    D. what record was borrowed

5. It is frequently helpful to file material under two subjects. In such a case the material is filed under one subject and a card indicating where the material is filed is placed under the other subject. This card is known generally as a

    A. follow-up or tickler card   B. guide card
    C. transfer card   D. cross-reference card

6. Of the following, for which reason are cross-references necessary in filing?

    A. there is a choice of terms under which the correspondence may be filed
    B. the only filing information contained in the correspondence is the name of the writer
    C. records are immediately visible without searching through the files
    D. persons other than file clerks can easily locate material

7. In filing, a clerk must often attach several papers together before placing them in the files. Usually, the MOST desirable of the following methods of attaching these papers is to

    A. pin them together
    B. staple them together
    C. attach them with a paper clip
    D. glue them together

8. A clerk employed in the central file section of a city department has been requested to obtain a certain card which is kept in an alphabetic file containing several thousand cards, The clerk finds that this card is not in its proper place and that there is no *out* card to aid him in tracing its location. Of the following, the course of action which would be LEAST helpful to him in locating the missing card would be for him to

    A. secure the assistance of his superior
    B. look at several cards filed immediately before and after the place where the missing card should be filed
    C. ask the other clerks in the file section whether they have this card
    D. prepare an *out* card and place it where the missing card should be filed

9. A clerk assigned to file correspondence in a subject file would be MOST concerned with the

    A. name of the sender
    B. main topic of the correspondence
    C. city and state of the sender
    D. date of the correspondence

10. Filing, in a way, is a form of recording. The one of the following which BEST explains this statement is that

    A. no other records are required if a proper filing system is used
    B. important records should, as a rule, be kept in filing cabinets
    C. a good system of record keeping eliminates the necessity for a filing system
    D. filing a letter or document is, in effect, equivalent to making a record of its contents

11. Of the following, a centralized filing system is LEAST suitable for filing

    A. material which is confidential in nature
    B. routine correspondence
    C. periodic reports of the divisions of the department
    D. material used by several divisions of the department

12. *A misplaced record is a lost record,* Of the following, the most valid implication of this statement in regard to office work is that

    A. all records in an office should be filed in strict alphabetical order
    B. accuracy in filing is essential
    C. only one method of filing should be used throughout the office
    D. files should be locked when not in use

13. Suppose that you are in charge of a unit which maintains a rather intricate filing system. A new file clerk has been added to your staff. Of the following assignments that may be given to this clerk, the one which requires the LEAST amount of knowledge of the filing system is

    A. placing material in the files
    B. removing papers from the files
    C. classifying and coding material for filing
    D. keeping a record of material taken from, and returned to, the files

14. Which one of the following is the MOST important objective of filing?

    A. Giving a secretary something to do in her spare time
    B. Making it possible to locate information quickly
    C. Providing a place to store unneeded documents
    D. Keeping extra papers from accumulating on workers' desks

15. Which one of the following BEST describes the usual arrangement of a tickler file?

    A. Alphabetical   B. Chronological
    C. Numerical   D. Geographical

16. Which one of the following is the LEAST desirable filing practice?

    A. Using staples to keep papers together
    B. Filing all material without regard to date
    C. Keeping a record of all materials removed from the files
    D. Writing filing instructions on each paper prior to filing

17. The *one* of the following records which it would be MOST advisable to keep in *alphabetical order* is a

    A. continuous listing of phone messages, including time and caller, for your supervisor
    B. listing of individuals currently employed by your agency in a particular title
    C. record of purchases paid for by the petty cash fund
    D. dated record of employees who have borrowed material from the files in your office

18. Assume that, in an office of a city agency, correspondence is filed, according to the date received, in 12 folders, one for each month of the year. On January 1 of each year, correspondence dated through December 31 of the preceding year is transferred from the active to the inactive files. New folders are then inserted in the active files to contain the correspondence to be filed in the next year. The one of the following which is the chief disadvantage of this method of transferring correspondence from active to inactive files is that

A. the inactive files may lack the capacity to contain all the correspondence transferred to them
B. the folders prepared each year must be labeled the same as the folders in preceding years
C. some of the correspondence from the preceding year may not be in the active files on January 1
D. some of the correspondence transferred to the inactive files may be referred to as frequently as some of the correspondence in the active files

19. The central filing unit of a certain city department keeps in its files records used by the various bureaus in connection with their daily work. It is desirable for the clerks in this filing unit to refile records as soon as possible after they have been returned by the different bureaus *CHIEFLY* because

    A. records which are needed can be located most easily if they have been filed
    B. such procedure develops commendable work habits among the employees
    C. records which are not filed immediately are ususally filed incorrectly
    D. the accumulation of records to be filed gives the office a disorderly appearance

20. The active and inactive file material of an office is to be filed in several four-drawer filing cabinets. Of the following, the BEST method of filing the material is, in general, to

    A. keep inactive material in the upper drawers of the file cabinet so that such material may be easily removed for disposal
    B. keep active material in the upper drawers so that the amount of stooping by clerks using the files is reduced to a minimum
    C. assign drawers in the file cabinets alternately to active and to inactive material so that file material can be transferred easily from the active to the inactive files
    D. assign file cabinets alternately to active and to inactive material so that cross-references between the two types of material can be easily made

---

KEY (CORRECT ANSWERS)

1.	B	11.	A
2.	A	12.	B
3.	B	13.	D
4.	C	14.	B
5.	D	15.	B
6.	A	16.	B
7.	B	17.	B
8.	D	18.	D
9.	B	19.	A
10.	D	20.	B

TEST 2

DIRECTIONS: Each question or incomplete statement is followed by several suggested answers or completions. Select the one that *BEST* answers the question or completes the statement. *PRINT THE LETTER OF THE CORRECT ANSWER IN THE SPACE AT THE RIGHT.*

1. Suppose you are checking an alphabetical card reference file to locate information about a *George Dyerly*. After checking all the *D's* you can find a card only for a *George Dyrely*. Of the following, the BEST action for you to take is to

    A. check the balance of the file to see if the card you are interested in has been misfiled
    B. check the data on the card to see if it relates to the same person in whom you are interested
    C. correct the spelling of the name on your records and reports to conform to the spelling on the card
    D. reject this reference file as a source of information regarding this person

2. Assume that you have been assigned by your supervisor to file some record cards in a cabinet. All the cards in this cabinet are supposed to be kept in strict alphabetical order. You know that important work is being held up because certain cards in this cabinet cannot be located. While filing the records given you, you come across a card which is not in its correct alphabetical place. Of the following, the BEST reason for you to bring this record to the attention of your supervisor is that

    A. errors in filing are more serious than other types of errors
    B. your alertness in locating the card should be rewarded
    C. the filing system may be at fault, rather than the employee who misfiled the card
    D. time may be saved by such action

3. A *tickler file* is used CHIEFLY for

    A. unsorted papers which the file clerk has not had time to file
    B. personnel records
    C. pending matters which should receive attention at some particular time
    D. index to cross-referenced material

4. A new file clerk who has not become thoroughly familiar with the files is unable to locate *McLeod* in the correspondence files under *Mc* and asks your help. Of the following, the BEST reply to give her is that

    A. there probably is no correspondence in the files for that person
    B. she probably has the name spelled wrong and should verify the spelling
    C. she will probably find the correspondence under *McLeod* as the files are arranged with the prefix *Mc* considered as *Mac* (as if the name were spelled *MacLeod*).
    D. the correspondence folder for *McLeod* has evidently been misplaced or borrowed from the files

5. Assume you are in an office which uses a subject filing system. You find that frequently a letter to be filed involves two or three subjects. In filing such a letter, it is MOST important to

    A. file it under the subject that is mentioned first in the letter
    B. prepare cross-references for the subjects covered in the letter

C. list all subjects involved on the label of the file folder
D. code the letter to show the main subject and its subdivisions

6. The MOST frequently used filing system in ordinary office practice is the

   A. alphabetic system
   B. numeric system
   C. geographic system
   D. subject system

7. If you wanted to check on the accuracy of the filing in your unit, you would

   A. check all the files thoroughly at regular intervals
   B. watch the clerks while they are filing
   C. glance through filed papers at random
   D. inspect thoroughly a small section of the files selected at random

8. The decision of a secretary to set up and maintain a subject filing system is MOST justified if

   A. speed in placing material in the files is of primary importance
   B. she is generally asked to obtain all the filed material dealing with a particular transaction or topic
   C. the system must be simple enough to permit its use by practically any employee with a little knowledge of filing
   D. there is to be no need to classify material before filing it

9. Several filing operaitons are performed by a secretary in operating and maintaining a subject filing system. Of the filing operations, the two which the secretary can MOST practicably perform at the same time are

   A. coding and placing material in the files
   B. classifying and placing material in the files
   C. placing material in the files and charging out borrowed material
   D. classifying and coding material for the files

10. Of the following systems of filing, the one that is considered the best for safeguarding confidential records is the

    A. alphabetical
    B. numerical
    C. geographical
    D. subject

11. While working in a clinic, you discover some obvious inconsistencies in the filing system as a whole. You also have in mind a corrective measure which you would like to see put into practice. The one of the following which is the MOST acceptable procedure for you to follow is to

    A. try out your new system for a few days to determine its success before discussing it with your supervisor
    B. explain the probable advantages of your proposed plan to your supervisor and secure his approval before making any changes
    C. continue working under the old procedure until the inconsistencies become apparent to the rest of the staff
    D. collect sufficient evidence to prove the obvious inconsistencies in the present filing system in order to convince your supervisor that the system is unsatisfactory

12. Assume that you are in charge of the patients' files in the health center to which you are assigned. The record cards of the individual patients are filed alphabetically according to the name of the patient. You want to make it easier to pick out the cards of those patients who are under treatment for any one of five indicated diseases. Of the following, the procedure which would be MOST helpful for this purpose would be to

    A. insert the card of each patient having one of the five diseases into a special folder
    B. use a different size card for each of the five diseases
    C. use a different color card for each of the five diseases
    D. underline the name of the disease on each card in the file

12._____

13. When papers are filed according to the date of their receipt, they are said to be filed

    A. numerically
    B. geographically
    C. chronologically
    D. alphabetically

13._____

14. The one of the following which is the MOST important requirement of a good filing system is that

    A. the expense of installation and operation be low
    B. papers be found easily when needed
    C. the system be capable of any amount of expansion which may be necessary in the future
    D. the filing system have a cross-reference index

14._____

15. The MAIN purpose of transferring materials from active to inactive files is to

    A. keep current reference files from growing to a size where they become inefficient and unmanageable
    B. distinguish between important business and less important matters
    C. provide a means of storing letters that need not be answered
    D. make sure that there is some way of retrieving information from previous years

15._____

16. The one of the following for which a cross-index is *most likely* to be needed is a

    A. file of reference material arranged by subject
    B. file of individual personnel records arranged alphabetically
    C. card file containing addresses and phone numbers for various organizations
    D. supervisor's *tickler file*

16._____

17. The CHIEF advantage of a rotary file is that

    A. it holds much more material than a standard file cabinet
    B. it provides a temporary location for material that is due to be placed in the permanent files
    C. items can be easily located and scanned without being removed from the file
    D. less time is required for placing an item on a rotary file than for placing it in a standard upright file

17._____

18. In a miscellaneous correspondence folder in a file drawer, it is *usually* MOST helpful if letters are arranged according to

    A. date with the most recent date on the bottom
    B. date with the most recent date on the top

18._____

C. subject with the subjects alphabetically arranged
D. name with the names arranged geographically

19. Assume that you are responsible for maintaining the patients' medical record file in the clinic to which you are assigned. Frequently, the other clinics in the health center where you work borrow record cards from your clinic files.
The BEST way for you to avoid difficulty in locating cards which may have been borrowed by other clinics is to

    A. make out a duplicate card for any clinic that wishes to borrow a card from your file
    B. refuse to lend your card to any other clinic unless the other clinic's personnel officer promises to return the card in person
    C. report it to your supervisor if anyone fails to return a card after a reasonable time
    D. have the person who borrows a card fill out an out-of-file card and place it in the file whenever a record card is removed

20. Suppose that you are given an unalphabetized list of 500 clinic patients and a set of unalphabetized record cards. Your supervisor asks you to determine if there is a record card for each patient whose name is on the list. For you to first arrange the medical record cards in alphabetical order BEFORE checking them with the names on the list is

    A. *desirable;* this will make it easier to check each name on the list against the patients' record cards
    B. *undesirable;* it is just as easy to alphabetize the names on the list as it is to rearrange the record cards
    C. *desirable;* this extra work with the record cards will give you more information about the patients
    D. *undesirable;* adding an extra step to the procedure makes the work too complicated

KEY (CORRECT ANSWERS)

1.	B	11.	B
2.	D	12.	C
3.	C	13.	C
4.	C	14.	B
5.	B	15.	A
6.	A	16.	A
7.	D	17.	C
8.	B	18.	B
9.	D	19.	D
10.	B	20.	A

TEST 3

DIRECTIONS: Each question or incomplete statement is followed by several suggested answers or completions. Select the one that *BEST* answers the question or completes the statement. *PRINT THE LETTER OF THE CORRECT ANSWER IN THE SPACE AT THE RIGHT.*

1. Of the following, for which reason are cross-references necessary in filing? 1.____

    A. There is a choice of terms under which the correspondence may be filed.
    B. The only filing information contained in the correspondence is the name of the writer.
    C. Records are immediately visible without searching through the files.
    D. Persons other than file clerks can easily locate material.

2. Suppose that the name files in your office contain filing guides on which appear the letters of the alphabet. The letters X, Y, and Z, unlike the other letters of the alphabet, are grouped together and appear on a single guide. Of the following, the BEST reason for combining these three letters into a single filing unit is probably that 2.____

    A. provision must be made for expanding the file if that should become necessary
    B. there is usually insufficient room for filing guides towards the end of a long file
    C. the letters X, Y, and Z are at the end of the alphabet
    D. relatively few names begin with these letters of the alphabet

3. You are requested by your supervisor to replace each card you take out of the files with an *out-of-file* slip. The *out-of-file* slip indicates which card has been removed from the file and where the card may be found. Of the following the CHIEF value of the *out-of-file* slip is that a clerk looking for a card which happens to have been removed by another clerk 3.____

    A. will know that the card has been returned to the file
    B. can substitute the *out-of-file* slip for the original card
    C. will not waste time searching for the card under the impression that it has been misfiled
    D. is not likely to misfile a card he has been using for some other purpose

4. Suppose that is is the practice, in your department, to file all the correspondence with one individual in a single folder and to file the most recent letters first in the folder. Of the following, the BEST justification for placing the most recent letter first rather than last in the folder is that, in general, 4.____

    A. letters placed in front of a folder are usually less accessible
    B. requests for previous correspondence from the files usually concern letters filed relatively recently
    C. letters in a folder can usually be lcoated most quickly when they are filed in a definite order
    D. filing can usually be accomplished very quickly when letters are placed in a folder without reference to date

5. While filing cards in an alphabetical file, you notice a card which is not in its correct alphabetical order. Of the following the BEST action for you take is to 5.____

    A. show the card to your supervisor and ask him whether that card has been reported lost

B. leave the card where it is, but inform the other clerks who use the file exactly where they may find the card if they need it
C. file a cross-reference card in the place where the card should have been filed
D. make a written notation of where you can find the card in the event that your supervisor asks you for it

6. A new alphabetical name card file covering fifteen file drawers has been set up in your office. Your supervisor asks you to place identifying labels outside each file drawer. Of the following, the BEST rule for you to follow in determining the appropriate label for each drawer is that

   A. the alphabet should be divided equally among the file drawers available
   B. each label should give the beginning and ending points of the cards in that drawer
   C. each drawer should begin with a new letter of the alphabet
   D. no drawer should contain more than two letters of the alphabet

7. One of the administrators in your department cannot find an important letter left on his desk. He believes that the letter may accidentally have been placed among a group of letters sent to you for filing. You look in the file and find the letter filed in its correct place. Of the following, the BEST suggestion for you to make to your supervisor in order to avoid repetition of such incidents is that

   A. file clerks should be permitted to read material they are requested to.
   B. correspondence files should be cross-indexed
   C. a periodic check should be made of the files to locate material inaccurately filed
   D. material which is sent to the file clerk should be marked *OK for filing.*

8. One of your duties is to keep a file of administrative orders by date. Your supervisor often asks you to find the order concerning a particular subject. Since you are rarely able to remember the date of the order, it is necessary for you to search through the entire file. Of the following, the BEST suggestion for you to make to your supervisor for remedying this situation is that

   A. each order bear conspicuously in its upper left hand corner the precise date on which it is issued
   B. old orders be taken from the file and destroyed as soon as they are superseded by new orders, so that the file will not be overcrowded
   C. an alphabetic subject index of orders be prepared so that orders can be located easily by content as well as date
   D. dates be eliminated entirely from orders

9. It is important that every office have a retention and disposal program for filing material. Suppose that you have been appointed administrative assistant in an office with a poorly organized records retention program. In establishing a revised program for the transfer or disposal of records, the step which would logically be taken THIRD in the process is

   A. preparing a safe and inexpensive storage area and setting up an indexing system for records already in storage
   B. determining what papers to retain and for how long a period
   C. taking an inventory of what is filed, where it is filed, how much is filed and how often it is used
   D. moving records from active to inactive files and destroying useless records

10. In evaluating the effectiveness of a filing system, the one of the following criteria which you should consider MOST important is the

    A. safety of material in the event of a fire
    B. ease with which material may be located
    C. quantity of papers which can be filed
    D. extent to which material in the filing system is being used

11. In a certain file room it is customary, when removing a record from the files, to insert an out card in its place. A clerk suggests keeping, in addition, a chronological list of all records removed and the names of the employees who have removed them. This suggestion would be of GREATEST value

    A. in avoiding duplication of work
    B. in enabling an employee to refile records
    C. where records are frequently misfiled
    D. where records are frequently kept out longer than necessary

12. You are given a large batch of correspondence and asked to obtain the folder on file for each of the senders of these letters. The folders in your file room are kept in numerical order and an alphabetic cross-index file is maintained. Of the following, the BEST procedure would be for you to

    A. look up the numbers in the alphabetic file, then alphabetize the correspondence according to the senders' names and obtain the folders from the numerical file
    B. alphabetize the correspondence according to the senders' names, get the file numbers from the alphabetic file and obtain the folders from the numerical file
    C. alphabetize the correspondence and then look through the numerical file for the proper folders in the order in which your correspondence is arranged
    D. look through the numerical file, pulling out the folders as you come across them

13. In filing terminology, coding means

    A. making a preliminary arrangement of names according to caption before bringing them together in final order of arrangement
    B. reading correspondence and determining the proper caption under which it is to be filed
    C. marking a card or paper with symbols or other means of identification to indicate where it is to be placed in the files according to a predetermined plan
    D. placing a card or paper in the files showing where correspondence may be located under another name or title

14. A duplex-number system of filing is a(n)

    A. decimal system
    B. arrangement of guides and folders with a definite color scheme to aid in filing and locating material
    C. system of filing by which classified subjects are divided and subdivided by number for the purpose of expansion
    D. method of filing names according to sound instead of spelling

15. A set of cards numbered from 1 to 300 has been filed in numerical order in such a way that the highest number is at the front of the file and lowest number is at the rear. It is desired that the cards be reversed to run in ascending order. The BEST of the following methods that can be used in performing this task is to

   A. begin at the front of the file and remove the cards one at a time, placing each one face up on top of the one removed before
   B. begin at the front of the file and remove the cards one at a time, placing each one face down on top of the one removed before
   C. begin at the back of the file and remove the cards in small groups, placing each group face down on top of the group removed before
   D. begin at the back of the file and remove the cards one at a time, placing each one face up on top of the one removed before

16. Confusion regarding the exact location of certain papers missing from files can probably BEST be avoided by

   A. using colored tabs
   B. using the Dewey Decimal System
   C. making files available to few persons
   D. consistently using *out* guides

17. The FIRST step in filing cards alphabetically is to

   A. count the cards
   B. divide the cards into groups of ten
   C. inspect each card to insure that it is filled out completely
   D. rearrange the cards in alphabetical order

18. If you cannot find the folder on Michael Hillston in an alphabetic file, you should

   A. assume that the folder is lost
   B. check other places where the folder could easily have been misfiled, like Hilston and Hillson
   C. look through all of the alphabetic files to see whether the folder was misplaced
   D. return to your other work and check for the folder again the next day

19. Of the following, the type of filing system used in the MOST efficiently run office depends *MOSTLY* on the

   A. way records are used or requested
   B. geographical location of the office
   C. skill of clerical personnel who do the filing
   D. number of filing clerks employed

20. The MOST important reason for well-organized files is to insure that

   A. business papers and records can easily be found
   B. company documents will be arranged alphabetically
   C. file space will be efficiently utilized for business purposes
   D. it is possible to identify the individual who committed any errors

KEY (CORRECT ANSWERS)

1.	A	11.	D
2.	D	12.	B
3.	C	13.	C
4.	B	14.	C
5.	A	15.	A
6.	B	16.	D
7.	D	17.	D
8.	C	18.	B
9.	A	19.	A
10.	B	20.	A

FILING

EXAMINATION SECTION

TEST 1

Questions 1-9.

DIRECTIONS: An important part of the duties of an office worker in a public agency is to file office records. Questions 1 through 9 are designed to determine whether you can file records correctly. Each of these questions consists of four names. For each question, select the one of the four names that should be FOURTH if the four names were arranged in alphabetical order. *PRINT THE LETTER OF THE CORRECT ANSWER IN THE SPACE AT THE RIGHT.*

1. A. 6th National Bank B. Sexton Lock Co. 1.____
   C. The 69th Street League D. Thomas Saxon Corp.

2. A. 4th Avenue Printing Co. B. The Four Corners Corp. 2.____
   C. Dr. Milton Fournet D. The Martin Fountaine Co.

3. A. Mr. Chas. Le Mond B. Model Express, Inc. 3.____
   C. Lenox Enterprises D. Mobile Supply Co.

4. A. Frank Waller Johnson B. Frank Walter Johnson 4.____
   C. Wilson Johnson D. Frank W. Johnson

5. A. Miss Anne M. Carlsen B. Mrs. Albert S. Carlson 5.____
   C. Mr. Alan Ross Carlsen D. Dr. Anthony Ash Carlson

6. A. Delaware Paper Co. B. William Del Ville 6.____
   C. Ralph A. Delmar D. Wm. K. Del Ville

7. A. The Lloyd Disney Co. B. Mrs. Raymond Norris 7.____
   C. Oklahoma Envelope, Inc. D. Miss Esther O'Neill

8. A. The Olympic Eraser Co. B. Mrs. Raymond Norris 8.____
   C. Oklahoma Envelope, Inc. D. Miss Esther O'Neill

9. A. Patricia MacNamara B. Eleanor McNally 9.____
   C. Robt. MacPherson, Jr. D. Helen McNair

Questions 10-21.

DIRECTIONS: Questions 10 through 21 are to be answered on the basis of the usual rules for alphabetical filing. For each question, indicate in the space at the right the letter preceding the name which should be THIRD in alphabetical order.

2 (#1)

10. A. Russell Cohen B. Henry Cohn 10.____
    C. Wesley Chambers D. Arthur Connors

11. A. Wanda Jenkins B. Pauline Jennings 11.____
    C. Leslie Jantzenberg D. Rudy Jensen

12. A. Arnold Wilson B. Carlton Willson 12.____
    C. Duncan Williamson D. Ezra Wilston

13. A. Joseph M. Buchman B. Gustave Bozzerman 13.____
    C. Constantino Brunelli D. Armando Buccino

14. A. Barbara Waverly B. Corinne Warterdam 14.____
    C. Dennis Waterman D. Harold Wartman

15. A. Jose Mejia B. Bernard Mendelsohn 15.____
    C. Antonio Mejias D. Richard Mazzitelli

16. A. Hesselberg, Norman J. B. Hesselman, Nathan B. 16.____
    C. Hazel, Robert S. D. Heintz, August J.

17. A. Oshins, Jerome B. Ohsie, Marjorie 17.____
    C. O'Shaugn, F.J. D. O'Shea, Frances

18. A. Petrie, Joshua A. B. Pendleton, Oscar 18.____
    C. Pertwee, Joshua D. Perkins, Warren G.

19. A. Morganstern, Alfred B. Morganstern, Albert 19.____
    C. Monroe, Mildred D. Modesti, Ernest

20. A. More, Stewart B. Moorhead, Jay 20.____
    C. Moore, Benjamin D. Moffat, Edith

21. A. Ramirez, Paul B. Revere, Pauline 21.____
    C. Ramos, Felix D. Ramazotti, Angelo

KEY (CORRECT ANSWERS)

1.	C	11.	B
2.	A	12.	A
3.	B	13.	D
4.	B	14.	C
5.	D	15.	C
6.	A	16.	A
7.	C	17.	D
8.	D	18.	C
9.	B	19.	B
10.	B	20.	B

21. C

TEST 2

DIRECTIONS: Each question or incomplete statement is followed by several suggested answers or completions. Select the one that BEST answers the question or completes the statement. *PRINT THE LETTER OF THE CORRECT ANSWER IN THE SPACE AT THE RIGHT.*

Questions 1-4.

DIRECTIONS: Questions 1 through 4 are to be answered on the basis of the following alphabetical rules.

RULES FOR ALPHABETICAL FILING

Names of Individuals

The names of individuals are filed in strict alphabetical order, *first* according to the last name, *then* according to first name or initial, and *finally* according to middle name or initial. For example: George Allen precedes Edward Bell and Leonard Reston precedes Lucille Reston.

When last names are the same, for example, A. Green and Agnes Green, the one with the initial comes before the one with the name written out when the first initials are identical.

Prefixes such as De, O', Mac, Mc and Van are filed as written and are treated as part of the names to which they are connected. For example, Gladys McTeaque is filed before Frances Meadows.

1. If the following four names were put into an alphabetical list, what would the FIRST name on the list be?
   A. Wm. C. Paul
   B. W. Paul
   C. Alice Paul
   D. Alyce Paule

1.____

2. If the following four names were put into an alphabetical list, what would the THIRD name on the list be?
   A. I. MacCarthy
   B. Irene MacKarthy
   C. Ida McCaren
   D. I.A. McCarthy

2.____

3. If the following four names were put into an alphabetical list, what would the SECOND name on the list be?
   A. John Gilhooley
   B. Ramon Gonzalez
   C. Gerald Gilholy
   D. Samuel Gilvecchio

3.____

4. If the following four names were put into an alphabetical list, what would the FOURTH name on the list be?
   A. Michael Edwinn
   B. James Edwards
   C. Mary Edwin
   D. Carlo Edwards

4.____

Questions 5-9.

DIRECTIONS: Questions 5 through 9 consist of a group of names which are to be arranged in alphabetical order for filing.

5. Of the following, the name which should be filed FIRST is
   A. Joseph J. Meadeen
   B. Gerard L. Meader
   C. John F. Madcar
   D. Philip F. Malder

6. Of the following, the name which should be filed LAST is
   A. Stephen Fischer
   B. Benjamin Fitchmann
   C. Thomas Fishman
   D. Augustus S. Fisher

7. The name which should be filed SECOND is
   A. Yeatman, Frances
   B. Yeaton, C.S.
   C. Yeatman, R.M.
   D. Yeats, John

8. The name which should be filed THIRD is
   A. Hauser, Ann
   B. Hauptmann, Jane
   C. Hauster, Mary
   D. Rauprich, Julia

9. The name which should be filed SECOND is
   A. Flora McDougall
   B. Fred E. MacDowell
   C. Juanita Mendez
   D. James A. Madden

Questions 10-14.

DIRECTIONS: Questions 10 through 14 are to be answered based on an alphabetical arrangement of the following list of names.

Walker, Carol J.	Wacht, Michael	Wade, Ethel
Wall, Fredrick	Wall, Francis	Wall, Frank
Wachs, Paul	Walker, Carol L.	Wagner, Arthur
Walters, Daniel	Wade, Ellen	Wald, William
Wagner, Allen	Walters, David	Walker, Carmen

10. The 4th name on the alphabetized list would be
    A. Wade, Ellen
    B. Wade, Ethel
    C. Wagner, Allen
    D. Wagner, Arthur

11. The 7th name on the alphabetized list would be
    A. Walker, Carmen
    B. Walker, Carol J.
    C. Walker, Carol L.
    D. Wald, William

12. The name that would come immediately AFTER Wagner, Arthur on the alphabetized list would be
    A. Wade, Ethel
    B. Wagner, Allen
    C. Wald, William
    D. Walker, Carol L.

13. The name that would come immediately BEFORE Wall, Frank would be   13.____
    A. Wall, Francis   B. Wall, Fredrick
    C. Walters, David   D. Walters, Daniel

14. The 12th name on the alphabetized list would be   14.____
    A. Walker, Carol L.   B. Wald, William
    C. Wall, Francis   D. Wall, Frank

KEY (CORRECT ANSWERS)

1.	C	6.	B	11.	D
2.	C	7.	C	12.	C
3.	A	8.	A	13.	A
4.	A	9.	D	14.	D
5.	C	10.	B		

TEST 3

DIRECTIONS: Each question or incomplete statement is followed by several suggested answers or completions. Select the one that BEST answers the question or completes the statement. *PRINT THE LETTER OF THE CORRECT ANSWER IN THE SPACE AT THE RIGHT.*

Questions 1-8.

DIRECTIONS: Questions 1 through 8 are based on the Rules of Alphabetical Filing given below. Read these rules carefully before answering the questions.

Names of People

1. The names of people are filed in strict alphabetical order, first according to the last name, then according to first name or initial, and finally according to middle name or initial. For example: George Allen comes before Edward Bell, and Leonard P. Reston comes before Lucille B. Reston.

2. When last names are the same, for example, A. Green and Agnes Green, the one with the initial comes before the one with the name written out when the first initials are identical.

3. When first and last names are alike and the middle name is given, for example, John David Doe and John Devoe Doe, the names should be filed in alphabetical order of the middle names.

4. When first and last names are the same, a name without a middle initial comes before one with a middle name or initial. For example, John Doe comes before John A. Doe and John Alan Doe.

5. When first and last names are the same, a name with a middle initial comes before one with a middle name beginning with the same initial. For example, Jack R. Hertz comes before Jack Richard Hertz.

6. Prefixes such as De, O', Mac, Mc, and Van are filed as written and are treated as part of the names to which they are connected. For example, Robert O'Dea is filed before David Olsen.

7. Abbreviated names are treated as if they were spelled out. For example: Chas. is filed as Charles and Thos. is filed as Thomas.

8. Titles and designations such as Dr., Mr., and Prof. are disregarded in filing.

Names of Organizations

1. The names of business organizations are filed according to the order in which each word in the name appears. When an organization name bears the name of a person, it is filed according to the rules for filing names of people as given above. For example: William Smith Service Co. comes before Television Distributors, Inc.

2 (#3)

2. Where bureau, board, office or department appears as the first part of the title of a governmental agency, that agency should be filed under the word in the title expressing the chief function of the agency. For example, Bureau of Budget would be filed as if written Budget, (Bureau of the). The Department of Personnel would be filed as if written Personnel, (Department of).

3. When the following words are part of an organization, they are disregarded: the, of, and.

4. When there are numbers in a name, they are treated as if they were spelled out. For example: 10th Street Bootery is filed as Tenth Street Bootery.

Each question from 1 through 8 contains four names numbered from 1 through 4 but not necessarily numbered in correct filing order. Answer each question by choosing the letter corresponding to the CORRECT filing order of the four names in accordance with the above rules.

SAMPLE QUESTION:
  I. Robert J. Smith
  II. R. Jeffrey Smith
  III. Dr. A. Smythe
  IV. Allen R. Smithers

A. I, II, III, IV   B. III, I, II, IV   C. II, I, IV, III   D. III, II, I, IV

Since the correct filing order, in accordance with the above rules is II I, IV, III, the correct answer is C.

1. I. J. Chester VanClief   II. John C. Van Clief
    III. J. VanCleve   IV. Mary L. Vance

    The CORRECT answer is:
    A. IV, III, I, II   B. IV, III, II, I   C. III, I, II, IV   D. III, IV, I, II

2. I. Community Development Agency   II. Department of Social Services
    III. Board of Estimate   IV. Bureau of Gas and Electricity

    The CORRECT answer is:
    A. III, IV, I, II   B. 1, II, IV, III   C. II, I, III, IV   D. I, III, IV, II

3. I. Dr. Chas. K. Dahlman   II. F. & A. Delivery Service
    III. Department of Water Supply   IV. Demano Men's Custom Tailors

    The CORRECT answer is:
    A. I, II, III, IV   B. I, IV, II, III   C. IV, I, II, III   D. IV, I, III, II

2 (#3)

4. I. 48th Street Theater II. Fourteenth Street Day Care Center 4._____
   III. Professor A. Cartwright IV. Albert F. McCarthy

   The CORRECT answer is:
   A. IV, II, I, III   B. IV, III, I, II   C. III, II, I, IV   D. III, I, II, IV

5. I. Frances D'Arcy II. Mario L. DelAmato 5._____
   III. William R. Diamond IV. Robert J. DuBarry

   The CORRECT answer is:
   A. I, II, IV, III   B. II, I, III, IV   C. I, II, III, IV   D. II, I, III, IV

6. I. Evelyn H. D'Amelio II. Jane R. Bailey 6._____
   III. Robert Bailey IV. Frank Baily

   The CORRECT answer is:
   A. I, II, III, IV   B. I, III, II, IV   C. II, III, IV, I   D. III, II, IV, I

7. I. Department of Markets 7._____
   II. Bureau of Handicapped Children
   III. Housing Authority Administration Building
   IV. Board of Pharmacy

   The CORRECT answer is:
   A. II, I, III, IV   B. I, II, IV, III   C. I, II, III, IV   D. III, II, I, IV

8. I. William A. Shea Stadium II. Rapid Speed Taxi Co. 8._____
   III. Harry Stampler's Rotisserie III. Wilhelm Albert Shea

   The CORRECT answer is:
   A. II, III, IV, I   B. IV, I, III, II   C. II, IV, I, III   D. III, IV, I, II

Questions 9-18.

DIRECTIONS: Questions 9 through 18 each show in Column I names written on four ledger cards (lettered w, x, y, z) which have to be filed. You are to choose the option (lettered A, B, C, or D) in Column II which BEST represents the proper order for filing the cards.

SAMPLE

COLUMN I COLUMN II
w. John Stevens A. w, y, z, x
x. John D. Stevenson B. y, w, z, x
y. Joan Stevens C. x, y, w, z
z. J. Stevenson D. x, w, y, z

3 (#3)

The correct way to file the cards is:
y. Joan Stevens
w. John Stevens
z. J. Stevenson
x. John D. Stevenson

The correct order is shown by the letters y, w, z, x in that sequence. Since, in Column II, B appears in front of the letters y, w, z, x in that sequence, B is the correct answer to the sample question.

Now answer the following questions, using the same procedure.

9. COLUMN I
w. Juan Montoya
x. Manuel Montenegro
y. Victor Matos
z. Victoria Maltos

   COLUMN II
   A. y, z, x, w
   B. z, y, x, w
   C. z, y, w, x
   D. y, x, z, w

   9._____

10. COLUMN I
w. Frank Carlson
x. Robert Carlson
y. George Carlson
z. Frank Carlton

    COLUMN II
    A. z, x, w, y
    B. z, y, x, w
    C. w, y, z, x
    D. w, z, y, x

    10._____

11. COLUMN I
w. Carmine Rivera
x. Jose Rivera
y. Frank River
z. Joan Rivers

    COLUMN II
    A. y, w, x, z
    B. y, x, w, z
    C. w, x, y, z
    D. w, x, z, y

    11._____

12. COLUMN I
w. Jerome Mathews
x. Scott A. Matthew
y. Charles B. Matthew
z. Scott C. Mathewsw

    COLUMN II
    A. w, y, z, x
    B. z, y, x, w
    C. z, w, x, y
    D. w, z, y, x

    12._____

13. COLUMN I
w. John McMahan
x. John P. MacMahan
y. Joseph DeMayo
z. Joseph D. Mayo

    COLUMN II
    A. w, x, y, z
    B. y, x, z, w
    C. x, w, y, z
    D. y, x, w, z

    13._____

14. COLUMN I
w. Raymond Martinez
x. Ramon Martinez
y. Prof. Ray Martinez
z. Dr. Raymond Martin

    COLUMN II
    A. z, x, y, w
    B. z, y, x, w
    C. z, w, y, x
    D. y, x, w, z

    14._____

15. COLUMN I   COLUMN II   15.____
    w. Mr. Robert Vincent Mackintosh   A. y, x, z, w
    x. Robert Reginald Macintosh   B. x, w, z, y
    y. Roger V. McIntosh   C. x, w, y, z
    z. Robert R. Mackintosh   D. x, z, w, y

16. COLUMN I   COLUMN II   16.____
    w. Dr. D. V. Facsone   A. y, w, z, x
    x. Prof. David Fascone   B. w, y, x, z
    y. Donald Facsone   C. w, y, z, x
    z. Mrs. D. Fascone   D. z, w, x, y

17. COLUMN I   COLUMN II   17.____
    w. Johnathan Q. Addams   A. z, x, w, y
    x. John Quincy Adams   B. z, x, y, w
    y. J. Quincy Addams   C. y, w, x, z
    z. Jerimiah Adams   D. x, w, z, y

18. COLUMN I   COLUMN II   18.____
    w. Nehimiah Persoff   A. w, z, x, y
    x. Newton Pershing   B. x, z, y, w
    y. Newman Perring   C. y, x, w, z
    z. Nelson Persons   D. z, y, w, x

KEY (CORRECT ANSWERS)

1. A	6. D	11. A	16. C
2. D	7. D	12. D	17. B
3. B	8. C	13. B	18. C
4. D	9. B	14. A	
5. C	10. C	15. D	

TEST 4

Questions 1-13.

DIRECTIONS: Each question from 1 through 13 contains four names. For each question, choose the name that should be FIRST if he four names are to be arranged in alphabetical order in accordance with the Rule for Alphabetical Filing of Names of People given below. Read this rule carefully. Then, for each question, mark your answer space with the letter that is next to the name that should be first in alphabetical order.

RULE FOR ALPHABETICAL FILING OF NAMES OF PEOPLE

The names of people are filed in strict alphabetical order, first according to the last name, then according to the first name. For example; George Allen comes before Edward Bell, and Alice Reston comes before Lucille Reston.

SAMPLE QUESTION
A. Roger Smith (2)
B. Joan Smythe (4)
C. Alan Smith (1)
D. James Smithe (3)

The number in parentheses show the proper alphabetical order in which these names should be filed. Since the name that should be filed FIRST is Alan Smith, the correct answer to the sample question is C.

1. A. William Claremont   B. Antonio Clements
   C. Anthony Clemente   D. William Claymont

2. A. Wayne Fumando   B. Sarah Femando
   C. Susan Fumando   D. Wilson Femando

3. A. Wilbur Hanson   B. Wm. Hansen
   C. Robert Hansen   D. Thomas Hanson

4. A. George St. John   B. Thomas Santos
   C. Frances Starks   D. Mary S. Stranum

5. A. Franklin Carrol   B. Timothy Carrol
   C. Timothy S. Carol   D. Frank F. Carroll

6. A. Christie-Barry Storage   B. John Christie-Barry
   C. The Christie-Barry Company D. Anne Christie-Barrie

7. A. Inter State Travel Co.   A. Interstate Car Rental
   C. Inter State Trucking   D. Interstate Lending Inst.

8. A. The Los Angeles Tile Co.
    B. Anita F. Los
    C. The Lost & Found Detective Agency
    D. Jason Los-Brio

    8.____

9. A. Prince Charles   B. Prince Charles Coiffures
    C. Chas. F. Prince   D. Thomas A. Charles

    9.____

10. A. U.S. Dept. of Agriculture   B. United States Aircraft Co.
    C. U.S. Air Transport, Inc.   D. The United Union

    10.____

11. A. Meyer's Art Shop   B. Frank B. Meyer
    C. Meyers' Paint Store   D. Meyer and Goldberg

    11.____

12. A. David Des Laurier   B. Des Moines Flower Shop
    C. Henry Desanto   D. Mary L. Desta

    12.____

13. A. Jeffrey Van Der Meer   B. Jeffrey M. Vander
    C. Jeffrey Van   D. Wallace Meer

    13.____

KEY (CORRECT ANSWERS)

1.	A	6.	D	11.	A
2.	B	7.	B	12.	C
3.	C	8.	B	13.	D
4.	A	9.	D		
5.	C	10.	C		

TEST 5

Questions 1-10.

DIRECTIONS: Questions 1 through 10 are to be answered on the basis of the usual rules of filing. Column I lists, next to the numbers 1 to 10, the names of 10 clinic patients. Column II lists, next to the letters A to D, the headings of file drawers into which you are to place the records of these patients. For each question, indicate in the space at the right the letter preceding the heading of the file drawer in which the record should be filed.

	COLUMN I		COLUMN II	
1.	Charles Coughlin	A.	Cab-Cep	1.____
2.	Mary Carstairs	B.	Ceq-Cho	2.____
3.	Joseph Collin	C.	Chr-Coj	3.____
4.	Thomas Chelsey	D.	Cok-Czy	4.____
5.	Cedric Chalmers			5.____
6.	Mae Clarke			6.____
7.	Dora Copperhead			7.____
8.	Arnold Cohn			8.____
9.	Charlotte Crumboldt			9.____
10.	Frances Celine			10.____

Questions 11-18.

DIRECTIONS: Questions 11 to 18 are to be answered on the basis of the usual rules of filing. Column I lists, next to the numbers 11 to 18, the names of 8 clinic patients. Column II lists, next to the letters A to O, the headings of file drawers into which you are to place the records of these patients. For each question, indicate in the space at the right the letter preceding the heading of the file drawer in which the record should be filed.

2 (#5)

COLUMN I	COLUMN II	
11. Thomas Adams	A. Aab-Abi	11._____
	B. Abj-Ach	
12. Joseph Albert	C. Aci-Aco	12._____
	D. Acp-Ada	
13. Frank Anaster	E. Adb-Afr	13._____
	F. Afs-Ago	
14. Charles Abt	G. Agp-Ahz	14._____
	H. Aia-Ako	
15. John Alfred	I. Akp-Ald	15._____
	J. Ale-Amo	
16. Louis Aron	K. Amp-Aor	16._____
	L. Aos-Apr	
17. Francis Amos	M. Aps-Asi	17._____
	N. Asj-Ati	
18. William Adler	O. Atj-Awz	18._____

Questions 19-28.

DIRECTIONS: Questions 19 through 28 are to be answered on the basis of the usual rules of filing. Column I lists, next to the numbers 19 through 28, the names of 10 clinic patients. Column II lists, next to the letters A to D the headings of file drawers into which you are to place the medical records of these patients. For each question, indicate in the space at the right the letter preceding the heading of the file drawer in which the record should be filed.

COLUMN I	COLUMN II	
19. Frank Shea	A. Sab-Sej	19._____
20. Rose Seaborn	B. Sek-Sio	20._____
21. Samuel Smollin	C. Sip-Soo	21._____
22. Thomas Shur	D. Sop-Syz	22._____
23. Ben Schaefer		23._____
24. Shirley Strauss		24._____
25. Harry Spiro		25._____
26. Dora Skelly		26._____
27. Sylvia Smith		27._____
28. Arnold Selz		28._____

KEY (CORRECT ANSWERS)

1.	D	11.	D	21.	C
2.	A	12.	I	22.	B
3.	D	13.	K	23.	A
4.	B	14.	B	24.	D
5.	B	15.	J	25.	D
6.	C	16.	M	26.	C
7.	D	17.	J	27.	C
8.	C	18.	E	28.	B
9.	D	19.	B		
10.	A	20.	A		

REPORT WRITING

EXAMINATION SECTION

TEST 1

DIRECTIONS: Each question or incomplete statement is followed by several suggested answers or completions. Select the one that BEST answers the question or completes the statement. *PRINT THE LETTER OF THE CORRECT ANSWER IN THE SPACE AT THE RIGHT.*

Questions 1-4.

DIRECTIONS: Answer Questions 1 through 4 on the basis of the following report which was prepared by a supervisor for inclusion in his agency's annual report.

Line #
1   On Oct. 13, I was assigned to study the salaries paid.
2   to clerical employees in various titles by the city and by
3   private industry in the area.
4   In order to get the data I needed, I called Mr. Johnson at
5   the Bureau of the Budget and the payroll officers at X Corp.—
6   a brokerage house, Y Co. —an insurance company, and Z Inc. —
7   a publishing firm. None of them was available and I had to call
8   all of them again the next day.
9   When I finally got the information I needed, I drew up a
10 chart, which is attached. Note that not all of the companies I
11 contacted employed people at all the different levels used in the
12 city service.
13 The conclusions I draw from analyzing this information is
14 as follows: The city's entry-level salary is about average for
15 the region; middle-level salaries are generally higher in the
16 city government plan than in private industry; but salaries at the
17 highest levels in private industry are better than city em-
18 ployees' pay.

1. Which of the following criticisms about the style in which this report is written is MOST valid?
    A. It is too informal.
    B. It is too concise.
    C. It is too choppy.
    D. The syntax is too complex.

    1._____

2. Judging from the statements made in the report, the method followed by this employee in performing his research was
    A. *good*; he contacted a representative sample of businesses in the area
    B. *poor*; he should have drawn more definite conclusions
    C. *good*; he was persistent in collecting information
    D. *poor*; he did not make a thorough study

    2._____

3. One sentence in this report contains a grammatical error. This sentence begins on line number
   A. 4   B. 7   C. 10   D. 14

4. The type of information given in this report which should be presented in footnotes or in an appendix is the
   A. purpose of the study
   B. specifics about the businesses contacted
   C. reference to the chart
   D. conclusions drawn by the author

5. The use of a graph to show statistical data in a report is SUPERIOR to a table because it
   A. features approximations
   B. emphasizes facts and relationships more dramatically
   C. presents data more accurately
   D. is easily understood by the average reader

6. Of the following, the degree of formality required of a written report in tone is MOST likely to depend on the
   A. subject matter of the report
   B. frequency of its occurrence
   C. amount of time available for its preparation
   D. audience for whom the report is intended

7. Of the following, a distinguishing characteristic of a written report intended for the head of your agency as compared to a report prepared for a lower-echelon staff member is that the report for the agency head should USUALLY include
   A. considerably more detail, especially statistical data
   B. the essential details in an abbreviated form
   C. all available source material
   D. an annotated bibliography

8. Assume that you are asked to write a lengthy report for use by the administrator of your agency, the subject of which is "The Impact of Proposed New Data Processing Operation on Line Personnel" in your agency. You decide that the *most* appropriate type of report for you to prepare is an analytical report, including recommendations.
   The MAIN reason for your decision is that
   A. the subject of the report is extremely complex
   B. large sums of money are involved
   C. the report is being prepared for the administrator
   D. you intend to include charts and graphs

9. Assume that you are preparing a report based on a survey dealing with the attitudes of employees in Division X regarding proposed new changes in compensating employees for working overtime. Three percent of the respondents to the survey voluntarily offer an unfavorable opinion on the method of assigning overtime work, a question not specifically asked of the employees.
On the basis of this information, the MOST appropriate and significant of the following comments for you to make in the report with regard to employees' attitudes on assigning overtime work is that
   A. an insignificant percentage of employees dislike the method of assigning overtime work
   B. three percent of the employees in Division X dislike the method of assigning overtime work
   C. three percent of the sample selected for the survey voiced an unfavorable opinion on the method of assigning overtime work
   D. some employees voluntarily voiced negative feelings about the method of assigning overtime work, making it impossible to determine the extent of this attitude

9._____

10. A supervisor should be able to prepare a report that is well-written and unambiguous.
Of the following sentences that might appear in a report, select the one which communicates MOST clearly the intent of its author.
   A. When your subordinates speak to a group of people, they should be well-informed.
   B. When he asked him to leave, SanMan King told him that he would refuse the request.
   C. Because he is a good worker, Foreman Jefferson assigned Assistant Foreman D'Agostino to replace him.
   D. Each of us is responsible for the actions of our subordinates.

10._____

11. In some reports, especially longer ones, a list of the resources (books, papers, magazines, etc.) used to prepare it is included. This list is called the
   A. accreditation   B. bibliography
   C. summary   D. glossary

11._____

12. Reports are usually divided into several sections, some of which are more necessary than others.
Of the following, the section which is ABSOLUTELY necessary to include in a report is
   A. a table of contents   B. the body
   C. an index   D. a bibliography

12._____

13. Suppose you are writing a report on an interview you have just completed with a particularly hostile applicant.
    Which of the following BEST describes what you should include in this report?
    A. What you think caused the applicant's hostile attitude during the interview
    B. Specific examples of the applicant's hostile remarks and behavior
    C. The relevant information uncovered during the interview
    D. A recommendation that the applicant's request be denied because of his hostility

14. When including recommendations in a report to your supervisor, which of the following is MOST important for you to do?
    A. Provide several alternative courses of action for each recommendation
    B. First present the supporting evidence, then the recommendations
    C. First present the recommendations, then the supporting evidence
    D. Make sure the recommendations arise logically out of the information in the report

15. It is often necessary that the writer of a report present facts and sufficient arguments to gain acceptance of the points, conclusions, or recommendations set forth in the report.
    Of the following, the LEAST advisable step to take in organizing a report, when such argumentation is the important factor, is a(n)
    A. elaborate expression of personal belief
    B. businesslike discussion of the problem as a whole
    C. orderly arrangement of convincing data
    D. reasonable explanation of the primary issues

16. In some types of reports, visual aids add interest, meaning, and support. They also provide an essential means of effectively communicating the message of the report.
    Of the following, the selection of the suitable visual aids to use with a report is LEAST dependent on the
    A. nature and scope of the report
    B. way in which the aid is to be used
    C. aid used in other reports
    D. prospective readers of the report

17. Visual aids used in a report may be placed either in the text material or in the appendix.
    Deciding where to put a chart, table, or any such aid should depend on the
    A. title of the report
    B. purpose of the visual aid
    C. title of the visual aid
    D. length of the report

18. A report is often revised several times before final preparation and distribution in an effort to make certain the report meets the needs of the situation for which it is designed.
    Which of the following is the BEST way for the author to be sure that a report covers the areas he intended?

A. Obtain a coworker's opinion
B. Compare it with a content checklist
C. Test it on a subordinate
D. Check his bibliography

19. In which of the following situations is an oral report preferable to a written report? When a(n)
    A. recommendation is being made for a future plan of action
    B. department head requests immediate information
    C. long-standing policy change is made
    D. analysis of complicated statistical data is involved

20. When an applicant is approved, the supervisor must fill in standard forms with certain information.
    The GREATEST advantage of using standard forms in this situation rather than having the supervisor write the report as he sees fit is that
    A. the report can be acted on quickly
    B. the report can be written without directions from a supervisor
    C. needed information is less likely to be left out of the report
    D. information that is written up this way is more likely to be verified

21. Assume that it is part of your job to prepare a monthly report for your unit head that eventually goes to the director. The report contains information on the number of applicants you have interviewed that have been approved and the number of applicants you have interviewed that have been turned down.
    Errors on such reports are serious because
    A. you are expected to be able to prove how many applicants you have interviewed each month
    B. accurate statistics are needed for effective management of the department
    C. they may not be discovered before the report is transmitted to the director
    D. they may result in loss to the applicants left out of the report

22. The frequency with which job reports are submitted should depend MAINLY on
    A. how comprehensive the report has to be
    B. the amount of information in the report
    C. the availability of an experienced man to write the report
    D. the importance of changes in the information included in the report

23. The CHIEF purpose in preparing an outline for a report is usually to insure that
    A. the report will be grammatically correct
    B. every point will be given equal emphasis
    C. principal and secondary points will be properly integrated
    D. the language of the report will be of the same level and include the same technical terms

6 (#1)

24. The MAIN reason for requiring written job reports is to
    A. avoid the necessity of oral orders
    B. develop better methods of doing the work
    C. provide a permanent record of what was done
    D. increase the amount of work that can be done

25. Assume you are recommending in a report to your supervisor that a radical change in a standard maintenance procedure should be adopted.
    Of the following, the MOST important information to be included in this report is
    A. a list of the reasons for making this change
    B. the names of others who favor the change
    C. a complete description of the present procedure
    D. amount of training time needed for the new procedure

KEY (CORRECT ANSWERS)

1.	A		11.	B
2.	D		12.	B
3.	D		13.	C
4.	B		14.	D
5.	B		15.	A
6.	D		16.	C
7.	B		17.	B
8.	A		18.	B
9.	D		19.	B
10.	D		20.	C

21. B
22. D
23. C
24. C
25. A

TEST 2

DIRECTIONS: Each question or incomplete statement is followed by several suggested answers or completions. Select the one that BEST answers the question or completes the statement. *PRINT THE LETTER OF THE CORRECT ANSWER IN THE SPACE AT THE RIGHT.*

1. It is often necessary that the writer of a report present facts and sufficient arguments to gain acceptance of the points, conclusions, or recommendations set forth in the report.
   Of the following, the LEAST advisable step to take in organizing a report, when such argumentation is the important factor, is a(n)
   A. elaborate expression of personal belief
   B. businesslike discussion of the problem as a whole
   C. orderly arrangement of convincing data
   D. reasonable explanation of the primary issues

   1.____

2. Of the following, the factor which is generally considered to be LEAST characteristic of a good control report is that it
   A. stresses performance that adheres to standard rather than emphasizing the exception
   B. supplies information intended to serve as the basis for corrective action
   C. provides feedback for the planning process
   D. includes data that reflect trends as well as current status

   2.____

3. An administrative assistant has been asked by his superior to write a concise, factual report with objective conclusions and recommendations based on facts assembled by other researchers.
   Of the following factors, the administrative assistant should give LEAST consideration to
   A. the educational level of the person or persons for whom the report is being prepared
   B. the use to be made of the report
   C. the complexity of the problem
   D. his own feelings about the importance of the problem

   3.____

4. When making a written report, it is often recommended that the findings or conclusions be presented near the beginning of the report.
   Of the following, the MOST important reason for doing this is that it
   A. facilitates organizing the material clearly
   B. assures that all the topics will be covered
   C. avoids unnecessary repetition of ideas
   D. prepares the reader for the facts that will follow

   4.____

5. You have been asked to write a report on methods of hiring and training new employees. Your report is going to be about ten pages long.
   For the convenience of your readers, a brief summary of your findings should
   A. appear at the beginning of your report
   B. be appended to the report as a postscript
   C. be circulated in a separate memo
   D. be inserted in tabular form in the middle of your report

6. In preparing a report, the MAIN reason for writing an outline is usually to
   A. help organize thoughts in a logical sequence
   B. provide a guide for the typing of the report
   C. allow the ultimate user to review the report in advance
   D. ensure that the report is being prepared on schedule

7. The one of the following which is MOST appropriate as a reason for including footnotes in a report is to
   A. correct capitalization
   B. delete passages
   C. improve punctuation
   D. cite references

8. A completed formal report may contain all of the following EXCEPT
   A. a synopsis
   B. a preface
   C. marginal notes
   D. bibliographical references

9. Of the following, the MAIN use of proofreaders' marks is to
   A. explain corrections to be made
   B. indicate that a manuscript has been read and approved
   C. let the reader know who proofread the report
   D. indicate the format of the report

10. Informative, readable, and concise reports have been found to observe the following rules:
    Rule I.   Keep the report short and easy to understand
    Rule II. Vary the length of sentences.
    Rule III. Vary the style of sentences so that, for example, they are not all just subject-verb, subject-verb.
    Consider this hospital laboratory report: The experiment was started in January. The apparatus was put together in six weeks. At that time, the synthesizing process was begun. The synthetic chemicals were separated. Then they were used in tests on patients.
    Which one of the following choices MOST accurately classifies the above rules into those which are violated by this report ad those which are not?
    A. II is violated, but I and III are not.
    B. III is violated, but I and II are not.
    C. II and III are violated, but I is not.
    D. I, II, and III are violated,

Questions 11-13.

DIRECTIONS: Questions 11 through 13 are based on the following example of a report. The report consists of eight numbered sentences, some of which are not consistent with the principles of good report writing.

(1) I interviewed Mrs. Loretta Crawford in Room 424 of County Hospital. (2) She had collapsed on the street and been brought into emergency. (3) She is an attractive woman with many friends judging by the cards she had received. (4) She did not know what her husband's last job had been, or what their present income was. (5) The first thing that Mrs. Crawford said was that she had never worked and that her husband was presently unemployed. (6) She did not know if they had any medical coverage or if they could pay the bill. (7) She said that her husband could not be reached by telephone but that he would be in to see her that afternoon. (8) I left word at the nursing station to be called when he arrived.

11. A good report should be arranged in logical order.
    Which of the following sentences from the report does NOT appear in its proper sequence in the report?
    A. 1   B. 4   C. 7   D. 8

12. Only material that is relevant to the main thought of a report should be included. Which of the following sentences from the report contains material which is LEAST relevant to this report? Sentence
    A. 3   B. 4   C. 6   D. 8

13. Reports should include all essential information.
    Of the following, the MOST important fact that is missing from this report is:
    A. Who was involved in the interview
    B. What was discovered at the interview
    C. When the interview took place
    D. Where the interview took place

Questions 14-15.

DIRECTIONS: Each of Questions 14 and 15 consists of four numbered sentences which constitute a paragraph in a report. They are not in the right order. Choose the numbered arrangement appearing after letter A, B, C, or D which is MOST logical and which BEST expresses the thought of the paragraph.

14. I.   Congress made the commitment explicit in the Housing Act of 1949, establishing as a national goal the realization of a decent home and suitable environment for every American family.
    II. The result has been that the goal of decent home and suitable environment is still as far distant as ever for the disadvantaged urban family
    III. In spite of this action by Congress, federal housing programs have continued to be fragmented and grossly under-funded.
    IV. The passage of the National Housing Act signaled a new federal commitment to provide housing for the nation's citizens.

The CORRECT answer is:
A. I, IV, III, II   B. IV, I, III, II   C. IV, I, III, II   D. II, IV, I, III

15.
  I. The greater expense does not necessarily involve "exploitation," but it is often perceived as exploitative and unfair by those who are aware of the price differences involved, but unaware of operating costs.
  II. Ghetto residents believe they are "exploited" by local merchants, and evidence substantiates some of these beliefs.
  III. However, stores in low-income areas were more likely to be small independents, which could not achieve the economies available to supermarket chains and were, therefore, more likely to charge higher prices, and the customers were more likely to buy smaller-sized packages which are more expensive per unit of measure.
  IV. A study conducted in one city showed that distinctly higher prices were charged for goods sold in ghetto stores than in other areas.

  The CORRECT answer is:
  A. IV, II, I, III   B. IV, I, III, II   C. II, IV, III, I   D. II, III, IV, I

16. In organizing data to be presented in a formal report, the FIRST of the following steps should be
  A. determining the conclusions to be drawn
  B. establishing the time sequence of the data
  C. sorting and arranging like data into groups
  D. evaluating how consistently the data support the recommendations

17. All reports should be prepared with at least one copy so that
  A. there is one copy for your file
  B. there is a copy for your supervisor
  C. the report can be sent to more than one person
  D. the person getting the report can forward a copy to someone else

18. Before turning in a report of an investigation he has made, a supervisor discovers some additional information he did not include in this report. Whether he rewrites this report to include this additional information should PRIMARILY depend on the
  A. importance of the report itself
  B. number of people who will eventually review this report
  C. established policy covering the subject matter of the report
  D. bearing this new information has on the conclusions of the report

KEY (CORRECT ANSWERS)

1. A
2. A
3. D
4. D
5. A

6. A
7. D
8. C
9. A
10. C

11. B
12. A
13. C
14. B
15. C

16. C
17. A
18. D

BASIC FUNDAMENTALS OF RECORD KEEPING

TABLE OF CONTENTS

	Page
Instructional Objectives	1
Content	1
Introduction	1
Filing Systems	2
Filing Methods	3
Miscellaneous Office Records	5
Data Processing	6
Processing the Data	6
Control Systems	7
Summary	8
Learning Activities	8
Management Activities	8
Evaluation Questions	9
Answer Key	10

BASIC FUNDAMENTALS OF RECORD KEEPING

Instructional Objectives
1. Ability to identify the characteristics of an effective record keeping system
2. Ability to explain the need for accurate, carefully maintained records in governmental agencies
3. Ability to identify the types of records that a governmental agency would maintain
4. Ability to develop a basic competence in alphabetical filing as well as an understanding of the variations in alphabetical filing rules and methods utilized in governmental agencies
5. Ability to recognize and utilize the various systems of filing in addition to (or in conjunction with) the alphabetical system
6. Ability to develop skill in finding information in office files, reference materials and agency manuals
7. Ability to develop a system of keeping track of the materials that have been removed from the files for study, microfilming or updating
8. Ability to describe the advantages of using microfilm for keeping records
9. Ability to analyze and determine the proper use of automated record keeping systems, such as the computer

Content

Introduction

From the birth certificate to the death certificate, everyone's lives are governed by records. The birth certificate verifies the individual's age, and will determine when he will enter public school, assume adult responsibilities and privileges, and be eligible to collect Social Security retirement benefits. School records will usually have direct bearing upon the individual's occupation. Federal and state income tax records will be established on the individual, as well as a record of marriage licenses, car licenses, and driver's licenses. This list of records ends with a death certificate which will enable the deceased's heirs to obtain his life insurance.

Public-service agencies, like individuals, are governed to a large extent by records of various sorts. Almost everyone who works in the field of public service will come in contact with different kinds of records and materials. Even the new employee may actually be involved in record keeping activities, or he may need to know about where different public records are kept, or how to find the necessary materials to assist in record keeping.

There is one basic reason for keeping or filing any records of valuable material – so that they may be found quickly when needed. In addition, there are basically two reasons for wanting to find materials – to verify or prove past actions or events, and to obtain information needed for planning future activities.

Materials to be filed in many public-service agencies may include letters, reports of many kinds (technical, financial, client interactions, marketing analyses), memorandums, copies of communications, contracts and other legal documents, price lists, clippings from newspapers and other published materials, checks, statements, receipts, bills, and other financial records.

One of the most important aspects of record keeping is the need for legibility. Records that cannot be read are of little value to anyone. Even though the intent of the author may be clear to himself, records are usually meant to be read by others as well. Often the author is not available for an on-the-spot interpretation. The importance of clear wording, good grammar, correct sentence structure, spelling, and proper paragraph structure cannot be overstated. For example, it is imperative that public-service financial records be kept accurately, clearly, and also legibly, since they are subject to audit at any time.

FILING SYSTEMS

Departmental Variances in Filing Needs: Governmental agencies have different departments, each with its various divisions, and often, separate filing systems. For example, the agency's personnel department might have its own filing system, divided into such unique categories as:
- Assignments
- Recruitment
- Training
- Classification
- Separation

Other departments, sections, or divisions would very probably also have filing systems unique to their own needs.

Basic Considerations of Systems: Thus, an effective record keeping system is organized with the programs and functions of the agency kept in mind. The filing system should be as simple as possible, and with accessibility to all clerical workers and members of the professional staff who must use it. A procedure for the periodic removal and disposal or storage of inactive records should be established. One person should be assigned responsibility for the maintenance of the files, with several individuals familiar enough to provide service during emergencies or vacation periods.

Another consideration in establishing a filing system is the security of the storage area from fire and vandalism. For example, school records and draft records have been frequent targets of vandals in recent years.

Filing Procedures: The first step in filing is to separate the materials to be filed from other office materials, inspect them for completeness, and to then determine which type of filing fits the need of that particular project. Some agencies follow a policy of having the responsible party initial the papers, with notes (such as dates) on action completed, and indicating that they are ready for filing. If this is the procedure, filing clerks should first check for the required initials, then read or skim the contents, to assist him when he is later asked to recall important papers. The next step would be to index the material, by mentally classifying it for its method and place of filing.

Manila folders are usually used to protect the papers. It is possible to obtain manila folders in various sizes, but the most common are letter size (8.5 x 11 inches) and legal size (8.5 x 13 inches). After the material has been filed into the cabinet, it is ready for future use.

Each file drawer should have sufficient guides or tabs to lead the eye to the desired section of the file quickly. The guide or tab may be:
- made of the material of the folder
- made of celluloid or other plastic
- made of metal with a plastic window

An angular tab slants back so that a worker does not have to bend over to read captions in lower drawers.

Filing Methods
While much of the detail of modern record keeping is accomplished by computers, there still exists a need for the traditional method of filing certain papers in office files.

Filing Alphabetically: Since this is the case, it is important that all office employees should know at least the basic rules of *alphabetical filing*. Some of the most commonly used filing rules are listed below. With an understanding of these rules, the beginning public-service worker should be able to maintain at least a semblance of order in a filing system:
- File papers by the last name (surname) – Example: Adams before Smith
- When the last names of two or more persons begin with the same first letter, look at the second letter in the names as your aid for selecting the name to be filed in front of the other. If the second letter is the same, then look at the third, and so on. – Example: Jackson before James
- File "nothing" before "something" – Example: Johns before Johnson
- If the last names (surnames) of two or more persons are the same, compare the first letters in the first names to help you decide the order of filing. If the first letters in the first names (given names) are the same, compare the second letters in the given names, and so forth. – Example: "Jones, James" before "Jones, John"
- When a name contains a first name and a middle name or initial, consider the middle name or initial only if the surnames and the given names or initials are alike. – Example: Peters, Anna Mae before Peters, Anna Maria
- The complete name of a person in a business name is considered in the same order as if it appeared by itself. – Example: Thomas, Robert H. Company
- Names of business firms which do not contain complete names of persons are filed according to their first words. If the first words are the same, the second words are considered, and so forth. – Example: J & R Company before Johnson Supply Company
- There are many departments, bureaus, and offices in our Federal Government. When indexing any of these, U.S. Government comes first, followed by the department, bureau, or office.
- State, county, city, and other political subdivisions are indexed under the political subdivision, then under the principal word in the name of the department or office.

Although alphabetical filing is the primary type of filing the beginning public service worker will use, there are other methods of filing with which he should become familiar. These methods include systems for *numeric, subject,* and *geographic* filing:

Filing by the Numeric Method: Numeric filing systems are so called because numbers are used as captions on the guide and folder tabs. Alphabetic systems are direct systems because a person can go directly to the file drawer and, by means of the name captions, file or find records. Numeric systems are indirect because, in most cases, before papers can be placed in or taken from the file drawer, the worker must refer to an alphabetic card index to find the number assigned to a name or subject.

Numeric filing systems can be used to advantage in many circumstances, like:
- where papers would group themselves around definite cases, contracts, or operations that are active for reasonably long but indefinite periods, and that require permanent and extensive cross reference;
- where a file is referred to by number rather than the name of the person involved; or
- in confidential situations where names can be concealed from those handling the files by the use of number captions.

In numeric filing, a number is assigned consecutively to each correspondent or subject that warrants an individual folder as these correspondents or subjects develop. A number once assigned is maintained until a correspondent no longer does business with the agency or company, or a subject ceases to exist. After a specified period, the number may be reassigned. All papers pertaining to the correspondent or subject are placed in the individual folder bearing the number assigned to that correspondent or subject.

A numeric system cannot be operated without a card index that will identify the assigned numbers. Each card contains the name of a correspondent or subject and the number of the folder that has been assigned.

The Social Security system operated by the federal government is based on a numeric filing idea. Schools and colleges have long utilized student numbers, and recently began to use Social Security numbers as the student identification number. Welfare cases have numbers assigned to them and the record keeping is greatly simplified as a result of this means of control. The *Dictionary of Occupational Titles (DOT)* assigns a number to all of the occupations listed.

Filing by Subject: Subject filing is the arrangement of records by names of topics or things rather than by names of people, companies, or locations. Government agencies might find it more convenient to use subject files for these purposes:
- to organize records that do not refer to the name of a person or organization;
- to organize correspondence that is more likely to be called for by its subject than by the name of the correspondent;
- to group records concerning the activities or products of an organization, such as advertising, sales, typewriters, adding machines, etc., so that all the records about one activity or product can be obtained immediately from the files; or
- to group together records that would otherwise fall into very small subdivisions.

Because subject files must meet the requirements of the individual situation, it is unlikely that any two subject files will be organized exactly the same. The nature of the concern would determine the main subject headings, and then subdivisions would be added as necessary.

Filing by Dewey Decimal System: The Dewey Decimal method of classifying information used in libraries, and familiar to most people, is a combination of the subject, numeric, and alphabetical filing systems.

Filing by Geographic Identities: Geographic filing relates to papers arranged in alphabetic order, with sub-listings by location, and then by name or subject. This method has particular advantage for those agencies in which the organization of files or records depends to a large degree on where things happened, or where they are located. As an example, police-department files would probably be organized first on the basis of geographic sections of the city, and then by number, subject, or by the name of the individual concerned in the file.

The specific geographic divisions used will be determined by the filing needs of the agency involved. The primary guides would bear the names of the most important geographic divisions occurring in the operations of the department. The secondary guides would then be used for subdivisions of the main geographic units, as well as for alphabetic sections of the geographic divisions and subdivisions.

MISCELLANEOUS OFFICE RECORDS

Although the type of records and/or the kind of record keeping would vary from office to office, students should be given an introduction to some of the basic records that most office workers would be required to keep, such as petty cash or revolving cash records, budget records, purchase requisitions, purchase orders, and reports.

The book *Clerical Record Keeping* gives a good summary of petty cash records. It provides a thorough study of the various forms that need to be filled out to keep a petty cash fund, and of the affiliated records. It also explains the roles of employees and employers in connection with the records.

The same source book gives a summary of budget records and purchase records. Although designed for the budget records of an individual or a family, the same principles could be utilized in setting up and in maintaining budget records for an office situation. The purchase records go into detail regarding such things as stock record cards, purchase requisition forms, record of goods expected forms, price quotation cards, purchase orders, purchase invoices, and the purchases journal. Although these are slanted toward the needs of a business, they provide an excellent background for understanding the agency's operations outlining its procedures and forms.

The average office worker should also be proficient in knowing how to keep a current and accurate account of the funds in the budget. Various manuals or methods are available which cover very adequately this area of operations.

Many public-service workers find themselves working with payroll records. They must compute the wages from the time shown on time cards, figure gross wages, figure overtime, determine deductions for social security and income tax, and as a result, net pay. The cumulative employee wage records must be kept current, and such forms and reports as withholding tax forms must be prepared at the end of the year.

DATA PROCESSING

Data processing frightens some people. Complicated equipment and procedures that few people can understand are the first things envisioned by the great mass of the population. In its simplest terms, however, data processing is not complicated. Data (which, as you know, is a plural type of word) means unorganized bits of knowledge; processing means to manipulate or to handle. Broadly speaking, therefore, *data processing is the systematizing of many facts into useful organized information.*

A necessary part of the data processing done by a governmental employee is the placing of facts and information into the appropriate order, and recording them in such an organized manner that they can then be readily retrievable or found. The ability to organize and file information has no value if the ability does not also provide for a system to readily find the information, and then to put it to use.

Obtaining and Recording the Data: Every governmental agency, regardless of its size, must process data in order to provide operational information for both the internal needs of management and the external needs of the public. The information provided and the method used to obtain information will vary with the type and size of the agency. The method used will depend upon the volume of data to be processed, the time available for processing the data, and the amount of money that can be spent.

Recording on Forms: Forms are often used to assist in recording data, which facilitates the use of the data in other operations. They are used to communicate data to other individuals or departments; to expedite the storing of data; to increase speed and accuracy in classifying, sorting, and computing data; and to assist in summarizing data so that the information can be easily read. All forms used should be designed to facilitate the processing of data to meet the specific needs of the agency that is using them.

Forms are by no means the only mechanical devices used by record keepers. Those in charge of the handling of forms, and responsible for the information contained on them, have devised and utilized literally hundreds of different methods whereby their work could be done more rapidly and more efficiently.

Mechanical Recorders: Typewriters, imprinting devices, computers, check protectors, time clocks, copying equipment, and duplicating equipment are all means of recording data by the use of mechanical equipment. Various types of calculators (rotary, printing, key-driven, or electronic) are machines that help us to compute data more quickly and accurately. The cash register, that is used almost everywhere goods or services are traded for money, is a mechanism combining the functions of recording, computing, and retrieving essential data.

PROCESSING THE DATA

Electronic-Data Computers: A computer can automatically put data into storage, hold the data there, and then retrieve the data whenever instructed to do so, without human intervention and at electronic speed.

In a computer system, a series of repetitive operations can be performed without human intervention and at high speed. The computer does this by following a series of detailed instructions, called a *program,* which is stored in the computer itself. This stored program tells the computer what data to process, what operations to perform with the data, and what to do with the results; for example, to *store* or *print* the processed information.

Computer Possibilities and Limitations: In addition to doing clerical and accounting work, a computer can also make routine decisions; that is, it can make a choice among alternatives. It can also take alternative courses of action. The computer itself, for example, can select which part of the program to follow, an operation known as *branching.* A computer can also repeat a sequence of instructions; this is known as *looping.*

But, no matter how advanced, or how sophisticated its electronics, a computer can work only with the facts and figures that are fed into it. Obviously then, if wrong information is fed into the computer, wrong results will come out of the machine. Even though the actual computational time is short, the material must be programmed into the machine.

CONTROL SYSTEMS

Surveys of files show that from 1 to 5 percent of records are misfiled, and half of those misfiled are never found. A misfile rate of 1 percent is usually considered normal, but the goal of a government agency is always no misfiled materials. The records of an arrest, a prisoner, or a student's academic record are too important to be lost and, if they should be, the undermining of public confidence in the department would severely weaken its effectiveness.

Even though the greatest possible care has been taken, a paper will occasionally be missing when needed. A few clues, therefore, for conducting systematic searches for missing data may not be inappropriate:

- Look through the folder thoroughly. The paper may have been placed out of order or may be sticking to another paper.
- Look between and under folders. Sometimes a paper is mistakenly placed between folders instead of into the proper folder, and subsequently, is pushed or slips to the bottom of the tray.
- Look under similar names or headings.
- Look for transposed names. A paper may be filed under a first or second name instead of the surname, or it may be filed under the subject's maiden name.
- Check the "out" folders or substitution cards to see who used it last.
- Look in the *To Be Filed, Pending,* or *Suspense* file trays or lists.
- Check for cross-references or related material to see if the paper has been filed there.

If, after a thorough search, the paper is still not located, alert the other workers in your office and make a note to place in the file to prevent someone else from making an extensive search. However, in a well-organized agency, it is seldom that records are lost.

Much time may be saved by establishing and using a control system. If a control system is used, the location of every piece of information is known at all times. There are several major methods of charging out materials, such as these:

- Use of an *out guide;* a stiff guide with the word *out* written on the top. It has a pocket on the front in which may be placed a requisition slip indicating the user, date, and material taken.

- Insertion of an *out folder* in the position of the borrowed folder; this is used to store new material until the regular one is returned.
- Placing of *substitution cards* in regular folder to indicate that material has been removed.

When material has been returned to the files, the out guides, out folders, or substitution cards should be removed from the file. The notations should be crossed out to indicate that the borrower has returned the material.

SUMMARY

Record keeping is an important function of *every governmental agency*. How it is done will be determined to a large extent by the function of the agency, and the manner in which its records will be used. The manuals published by the agency will usually have detailed instructions covering maintaining of records; however, the people involved need to completely know the procedures, so that time is not wasted consulting the manual every time something is to be filed.

Anyone can stick papers into a file cabinet; however, responsibility does not end there. *The record must be available when needed.* This demands a thorough knowledge of the steps to follow in preparing materials to be filed and the various types of filing and record keeping systems.

LEARNING ACTIVITIES

- Prepare discussion notes on the characteristics of an excellent record keeping system
- Prepare an outline of the various types of classifying information for filing or storage
- Prepare an outline of the rules for alphabetizing material
- Alphabetize the set of index cards prepared by the instructor
- Prepare an outline of the procedures for establishing or using a numerical file
- Each trainee should prepare an organizational or functional chart of the department in which he wishes to work and indicate which records would need to be kept in each of the areas on the chart
- Visit a governmental agency and prepare a report on the record system used. Be sure to note such special problems as classifying and keeping records on fingerprints for future reference.

MANAGEMENT ACTIVITIES

- Prepare a bulletin board illustration of the various types of filing
- Obtain or prepare a set of index cards of the names of individuals, various governmental agencies, and departments which may be used to illustrate filing procedures
- Make a study of the records kept at the local governmental agencies and prepare material for discussion on the why's, how's, and procedures used by the various departments
- Make arrangements to visit a governmental office that utilizes all of the various record keeping devices
- Prepare a discussion on the rules for the alphabetical filing of material
- Obtain the budgetary forms from a governmental office and duplicate some of the simpler forms

- Prepare some simple budgetary problems. Let the class work on them in small groups.
- Prepare a discussion on the rules for the alphabetical filing of material
- Make arrangements with the librarian to demonstrate cross filing
- Encourage the staff to study on their own by reading programmed instruction books on record keeping and data processing
- Arrange for a debate on the advantages and disadvantages of using automated record keeping systems.
- Prepare discussion notes on what to do if some filed matter is lost
- Prepare group activities centered around the problem of keeping inactive files

EVALUATION QUESTIONS

1. Which one is not a basic reason for keeping records?   1._____
    A. To prove past actions
    B. To keep the staff working hard
    C. To obtain information for the present
    D. To help in planning for the future

2. Which statement is untrue?   2._____
    A. The filing system should be as simple as possible
    B. The filing system should be easily reached by those who use it
    C. Care should be taken that nothing is ever taken out of the filing system
    D. Care should be taken to keep the records storage area safe from fire and vandalism

3. If an agency has collected many papers on one topic or thing, it may use   3._____
which filing system?
    A. A subject system
    B. A geographic system
    C. A numeric system
    D. The Dewey Decimal System

4. Which type of filing is the Dewey Decimal System based on?   4._____
    A. Alphabetical
    B. Subject
    C. Numeric
    D. All of the above

5. The first step in filing is to: 5._____
    A. Index the material
    B. Separate the materials from other office material
    C. Inspect them for completeness
    D. Determine which type of filing is best

6. Data processing by public service workers means:
    A. Gathering together unorganized bits of knowledge
    B. Classifying knowledge
    C. Recording knowledge in an organized manner
    D. All of the above

7. Which statement is not true about computers?
    A. Information is able to be processed at increasing speeds as computers evolve technologically
    B. A computer can store data and retrieve it when instructed to do so
    C. A computer will not store data that includes wrong information
    D. A computer can do many operations without human beings and at high speed

8. If you were looking for a misfiled record it would be wise to:
    A. Look through the folder thoroughly
    B. Check the "out" folders or substitution cards to see who had it last
    C. Look in the "To Be Filed" or "Being Microfilmed" trays
    D. All of the above

Answer Key

1. B   4. D   7. C
2. C   5. B   8. D
3. A   6. D

PHILOSOPHY, PRINCIPLES, PRACTICES, AND TECHNICS
OF
SUPERVISION, ADMINISTRATION, MANAGEMENT, AND ORGANIZATION

TABLE OF CONTENTS

	Page
MEANING OF SUPERVISION	1
THE OLD AND THE NEW SUPERVISION	1
THE EIGHT (8) BASIC PRINCIPLES OF THE NEW SUPERVISION	1
I. Principle of Responsibility	1
II. Principle of Authority	2
III. Principle of Self-Growth	2
IV. Principle of Individual Worth	2
V. Principle of Creative Leadership	2
VI. Principle of Success and Failure	2
VII. Principle of Science	3
VIII. Principle of Cooperation	3
WHAT IS ADMINISTRATION?	3
I. Practices Commonly Classed as "Supervisory"	3
II. Practices Commonly Classed as "Administrative"	3
III. Practices Commonly Classed as Both "Supervisory" and "Administrative"	4
RESPONSIBILITIES OF THE SUPERVISOR	4
COMPETENCIES OF THE SUPERVISOR	4
THE PROFESSIONAL SUPERVISOR-EMPLOYEE RELATIONSHIP	4
MINI-TEXT IN SUPERVISION, ADMINISTRATION, MANAGEMENT, AND ORGANIZATION	5
I. Brief Highlights	5
A. Levels of Management	6
B. What the Supervisor Must Learn	6
C. A Definition of Supervision	6
D. Elements of the Team Concept	6
E. Principles of Organization	6
F. The Four Important Parts of Every Job	7
G. Principles of Delegation	7
H. Principles of Effective Communications	7
I. Principles of Work Improvement	7
J. Areas of Job Improvement	7
K. Seven Key Points in Making Improvements	8

	L.	Corrective Techniques for Job Improvement	8
	M.	A Planning Checklist	8
	N.	Five Characteristics of Good Directions	9
	O.	Types of Directions	9
	P.	Controls	9
	Q.	Orienting the New Employee	9
	R.	Checklist for Orienting New Employees	9
	S.	Principles of Learning	10
	T.	Causes of Poor Performance	10
	U.	Four Major Steps in On-the-Job Instructions	10
	V.	Employees Want Five Things	10
	W.	Some Don'ts in Regard to Praise	11
	X.	How to Gain Your Workers' Confidence	11
	Y.	Sources of Employee Problems	11
	Z.	The Supervisor's Key to Discipline	11
	AA.	Five Important Processes of Management	12
	BB.	When the Supervisor Fails to Plan	12
	CC.	Fourteen General Principles of Management	12
	DD.	Change	12
II.	Brief Topical Summaries		13
	A.	Who/What is the Supervisor?	13
	B.	The Sociology of Work	13
	C.	Principles and Practices of Supervision	14
	D.	Dynamic Leadership	14
	E.	Processes for Solving Problems	15
	F.	Training for Results	15
	G.	Health, Safety, and Accident Prevention	16
	H.	Equal Employment Opportunity	16
	I.	Improving Communications	16
	J.	Self-Development	17
	K.	Teaching and Training	17
		1. The Teaching Process	17
		a. Preparation	17
		b. Presentation	18
		c. Summary	18
		d. Application	18
		e. Evaluation	18
		2. Teaching Methods	18
		a. Lecture	18
		b. Discussion	18
		c. Demonstration	19
		d. Performance	19
		e. Which Method to Use	19

PHILOSOPHY, PRINCIPLES, PRACTICES, AND TECHNICS OF SUPERVISION, ADMINISTRATION, MANAGEMENT, AND ORGANIZATION

MEANING OF SUPERVISION

The extension of the democratic philosophy has been accompanied by an extension in the scope of supervision. Modern leaders and supervisors no longer think of supervision in the narrow sense of being confined chiefly to visiting employees, supplying materials, or rating the staff. They regard supervision as being intimately related to all the concerned agencies of society, they speak of the supervisor's function in terms of "growth," rather than the "improvement" of employees.

This modern concept of supervision may be defined as follows: Supervision is leadership and the development of leadership within groups which are cooperatively engaged in inspection, research, training, guidance, and evaluation.

THE OLD AND THE NEW SUPERVISION

TRADITIONAL
1. Inspection
2. Focused on the employee
3. Visitation
4. Random and haphazard
5. Imposed and authoritarian
6. One person usually

MODERN
1. Study and analysis
2. Focused on aims, materials, methods, supervisors, employees, environment
3. Demonstrations, intervisitation, workshops, directed reading, bulletins, etc.
4. Definitely organized and planned (scientific)
5. Cooperative and democratic
6. Many persons involved (creative)

THE EIGHT (8) BASIC PRINCIPLES OF THE NEW SUPERVISION

I. Principle of Responsibility
    Authority to act and responsibility for acting must be joined.
    A. If you give responsibility, give authority.
    B. Define employee duties clearly.
    C. Protect employees from criticism by others.
    D. Recognize the rights as well as obligations of employees.
    E. Achieve the aims of a democratic society insofar as it is possible within the area of your work.
    F. Establish a situation favorable to training and learning.
    G. Accept ultimate responsibility for everything done in your section, unit, office, division, department.
    H. Good administration and good supervision are inseparable.

II. Principle of Authority
The success of the supervisor is measured by the extent to which the power of authority is not used.
   A. Exercise simplicity and informality in supervision
   B. Use the simplest machinery of supervision
   C. If it is good for the organization as a whole, it is probably justified.
   D. Seldom be arbitrary or authoritative.
   E. Do not base your work on the power of position or of personality.
   F. Permit and encourage the free expression of opinions.

III. Principle of Self-Growth
The success of the supervisor is measured by the extent to which, and the speed with which, he is no longer needed.
   A. Base criticism on principles, not on specifics.
   B. Point out higher activities to employees.
   C. Train for self-thinking by employees to meet new situations.
   D. Stimulate initiative, self-reliance, and individual responsibility
   E. Concentrate on stimulating the growth of employees rather than on removing defects.

IV. Principle of Individual Worth
Respect for the individual is a paramount consideration in supervision.
   A. Be human and sympathetic in dealing with employees.
   B. Don't nag about things to be done.
   C. Recognize the individual differences among employees and seek opportunities to permit best expression of each personality.

V. Principle of Creative Leadership
The best supervision is that which is not apparent to the employee.
   A. Stimulate, don't drive employees to creative action.
   B. Emphasize doing good things.
   C. Encourage employees to do what they do best.
   D. Do not be too greatly concerned with details of subject or method.
   E. Do not be concerned exclusively with immediate problems and activities.
   F. Reveal higher activities and make them both desired and maximally possible.
   G. Determine procedures in the light of each situation but see that these are derived from a sound basic philosophy.
   H. Aid, inspire, and lead so as to liberate the creative spirit latent in all good employees.

VI. Principle of Success and Failure
There are no unsuccessful employees, only unsuccessful supervisors who have failed to give proper leadership.
   A. Adapt suggestions to the capacities, attitudes, and prejudices of employees.
   B. Be gradual, be progressive, be persistent.
   C. Help the employee find the general principle; have the employee apply his own problem to the general principle.
   D. Give adequate appreciation for good work and honest effort.
   E. Anticipate employee difficulties and help to prevent them.
   F. Encourage employees to do the desirable things they will do anyway.
   G. Judge your supervision by the results it secures.

VII. Principle of Science
Successful supervision is scientific, objective, and experimental. It is based on facts, not on prejudices.
   A. Be cumulative in results.
   B. Never divorce your suggestions from the goals of training.
   C. Don't be impatient of results.
   D. Keep all matters on a professional, not a personal, level.
   E. Do not be concerned exclusively with immediate problems and activities.
   F. Use objective means of determining achievement and rating where possible.

VIII. Principle of Cooperation
Supervision is a cooperative enterprise between supervisor and employee.
   A. Begin with conditions as they are.
   B. Ask opinions of all involved when formulating policies.
   C. Organization is as good as its weakest link.
   D. Let employees help to determine policies and department programs.
   E. Be approachable and accessible—physically and mentally.
   F. Develop pleasant social relationships.

WHAT IS ADMINISTRATION

Administration is concerned with providing the environment, the material facilities, and the operational procedures that will promote the maximum growth and development of supervisors and employees. (Organization is an aspect and a concomitant of administration.)

There is no sharp line of demarcation between supervision and administration; these functions are intimately interrelated and, often, overlapping. They are complementary activities.

I. Practices Commonly Classed as "Supervisory"
   A. Conducting employees' conferences
   B. Visiting sections, units, offices, divisions, departments
   C. Arranging for demonstrations
   D. Examining plans
   E. Suggesting professional reading
   F. Interpreting bulletins
   G. Recommending in-service training courses
   H. Encouraging experimentation
   I. Appraising employee morale
   J. Providing for intervisitation

II. Practices Commonly Classified as "Administrative"
   A. Management of the office
   B. Arrangement of schedules for extra duties
   C. Assignment of rooms or areas
   D. Distribution of supplies
   E. Keeping records and reports
   F. Care of audio-visual materials
   G. Keeping inventory records
   H. Checking record cards and books

    I.   Programming special activities
    J.   Checking on the attendance and punctuality of employees

III.   Practices Commonly Classified as Both "Supervisory" and "Administrative"
    A.   Program construction
    B.   Testing or evaluating outcomes
    C.   Personnel accounting
    D.   Ordering instructional materials

RESPONSIBILITIES OF THE SUPERVISOR

A person employed in a supervisory capacity must constantly be able to improve his own efficiency and ability. He represent the employer to the employees and only continuous self-examination can make him a capable supervisor.

Leadership and training are the supervisor's responsibility. An efficient working unit is one in which the employees work with the supervisor. It is his job to bring out the best in his employees. He must always be relaxed, courteous, and calm in his association with his employees. Their feelings are important, and a harsh attitude does not develop the most efficient employees.

COMPETENCES OF THE SUPERVISOR

    I.   Complete knowledge of the duties and responsibilities of his position.
    II.   To be able to organize a job, plan ahead, and carry through.
    III.   To have self-confidence and initiative.
    IV.   To be able to handle the unexpected situation and make quick decisions.
    V.   To be able to properly train subordinates in the positions they are best suited for.
    VI.   To be able to keep good human relations among his subordinates.
    VII.   To be able to keep good human relations between his subordinates and himself and to earn their respect and trust.

THE PROFESSIONAL SUPERVISOR-EMPLOYEE RELATIONSHIP

There are two kinds of efficiency: one kind is only apparent and is produced in organizations through the exercise of mere discipline; this is but a simulation of the second, or true, efficiency which springs from spontaneous cooperation. If you are a manager, no matter how great or small your responsibility, it is your job, in the final analysis, to create and develop this involuntary cooperation among the people whom you supervise. For, no matter how powerful a combination of money, machines, and materials a company may have, this is a dead and sterile thing without a team of willing, thinking, and articulate people to guide it.

The following 21 points are presented as indicative of the exemplary basic relationship that should exist between supervisor and employee:

1.   Each person wants to be liked and respected by his fellow employee and wants to be treated with consideration and respect by his superior.
2.   The most competent employee will make an error. However, in a unit where good relations exist between the supervisor and his employees, tenseness and fear do not exist. Thus, errors are not hidden or covered up, and the efficiency of a unit is not impaired.

3. Subordinates resent rules, regulations, or orders that are unreasonable or unexplained.
4. Subordinates are quick to resent unfairness, harshness, injustices, and favoritism.
5. An employee will accept responsibility if he knows that he will be complimented for a job well done, and not too harshly chastised for failure; that his supervisor will check the cause of the failure, and, if it was the supervisor's fault, he will assume the blame therefore. If it was the employee's fault, his supervisor will explain the correct method or means of handling the responsibility.
6. An employee wants to receive credit for a suggestion he has made, that is used. If a suggestion cannot be used, the employee is entitled to an explanation. The supervisor should not say "no" and close the subject.
7. Fear and worry slow up a worker's ability. Poor working environment can impair his physical and mental health. A good supervisor avoids forceful methods, threats, and arguments to get a job done.
8. A forceful supervisor is able to train his employees individually and as a team, and is able to motivate them in the proper channels.
9. A mature supervisor is able to properly evaluate his subordinates and to keep them happy and satisfied.
10. A sensitive supervisor will never patronize his subordinates.
11. A worthy supervisor will respect his employees' confidences.
12. Definite and clear-cut responsibilities should be assigned to each executive.
13. Responsibility should always be coupled with corresponding authority.
14. No change should be made in the scope or responsibilities of a position without a definite understanding to that effect on the part of all persons concerned.
15. No executive or employee, occupying a single position in the organization, should be subject to definite orders from more than one source.
16. Orders should never be given to subordinates over the head of a responsible executive. Rather than do this, the officer in question should be supplanted.
17. Criticisms of subordinates should, whoever possible, be made privately, and in no case should a subordinate be criticized in the presence of executives or employees of equal or lower rank.
18. No dispute or difference between executives or employees as to authority or responsibilities should be considered too trivial for prompt and careful adjudication.
19. Promotions, wage changes, and disciplinary action should always be approved by the executive immediately superior to the one directly responsible.
20. No executive or employee should ever be required, or expected, to be at the same time an assistant to, and critic of, another.
21. Any executive whose work is subject to regular inspection should, wherever practicable, be given the assistance and facilities necessary to enable him to maintain an independent check of the quality of his work.

MINI-TEXT IN SUPERVISION, ADMINISTRATION, MANAGEMENT, AND ORGANIZATION

I. Brief Highlights

Listed concisely and sequentially are major headings and important data in the field for quick recall and review.

A. Levels of Management
Any organization of some size has several levels of management. In terms of a ladder, the levels are:

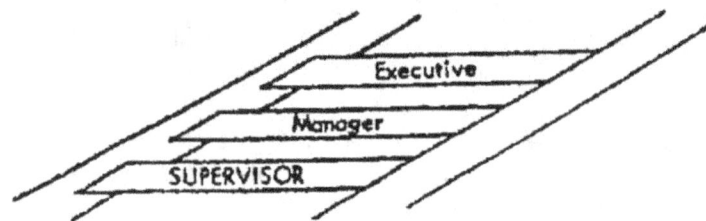

The first level is very important because it is the beginning point of management leadership.

B. What the Supervisor Must Learn
A supervisor must learn to:
1. Deal with people and their differences
2. Get the job done through people
3. Recognize the problems when they exist
4. Overcome obstacles to good performance
5. Evaluate the performance of people
6. Check his own performance in terms of accomplishment

C. A Definition of Supervisor
The term supervisor means any individual having authority, in the interests of the employer, to hire, transfer, suspend, lay-off, recall, promote, discharge, assign, reward, or discipline other employees or responsibility to direct them, or to adjust their grievances, or effectively to recommend such action, if, in connection with the foregoing, exercise of such authority is not of a merely routine or clerical nature but requires the use of independent judgment.

D. Elements of the Team Concept
What is involved in teamwork? The component parts are:
1. Members
2. A leader
3. Goals
4. Plans
5. Cooperation
6. Spirit

E. Principles of Organization
1. A team member must know what his job is.
2. Be sure that the nature and scope of a job are understood.
3. Authority and responsibility should be carefully spelled out.
4. A supervisor should be permitted to make the maximum number of decisions affecting his employees.
5. Employees should report to only one supervisor.
6. A supervisor should direct only as many employees as he can handle effectively.
7. An organization plan should be flexible.

8. Inspection and performance of work should be separate.
9. Organizational problems should receive immediate attention.
10. Assign work in line with ability and experience.

F. The Four Important Parts of Every Job
1. Inherent in every job is the *accountability* for results.
2. A second set of factors in every job is *responsibilities*.
3. Along with duties and responsibilities one must have the *authority* to act within certain limits without obtaining permission to proceed.
4. No job exists in a vacuum. The supervisor is surrounded by key *relationships*.

G. Principles of Delegation
Where work is delegated for the first time, the supervisor should think in terms of these questions:
1. Who is best qualified to do this?
2. Can an employee improve his abilities by doing this?
3. How long should an employee spend on this?
4. Are there any special problems for which he will need guidance?
5. How broad a delegation can I make?

H. Principles of Effective Communications
1. Determine the media.
2. To whom directed?
3. Identification and source authority.
4. Is communication understood?

I. Principles of Work Improvement
1. Most people usually do only the work which is assigned to them.
2. Workers are likely to fit assigned work into the time available to perform it.
3. A good workload usually stimulates output.
4. People usually do their best work when they know that results will be reviewed or inspected.
5. Employees usually feel that someone else is responsible for conditions of work, workplace layout, job methods, type of tools/equipment, and other such factors.
6. Employees are usually defensive about their job security.
7. Employees have natural resistance to change.
8. Employees can support or destroy a supervisor.
9. A supervisor usually earns the respect of his people through his personal example of diligence and efficiency.

J. Areas of Job Improvement
The areas of job improvement are quite numerous, but the most common ones which a supervisor can identify and utilize are:
1. Departmental layout
2. Flow of work
3. Workplace layout
4. Utilization of manpower
5. Work methods
6. Materials handling

7. Utilization
8. Motion economy

K. Seven Key Points in Making Improvements
1. Select the job to be improved
2. Study how it is being done now
3. Question the present method
4. Determine actions to be taken
5. Chart proposed method
6. Get approval and apply
7. Solicit worker participation

I. Corrective Techniques of Job Improvement
Specific Problems
1. Size of workload
2. Inability to meet schedules
3. Strain and fatigue
4. Improper use of men and skills
5. Waste, poor quality, unsafe conditions
6. Bottleneck conditions that hinder output
7. Poor utilization of equipment and machine
8. Efficiency and productivity of labor

General Improvement
1. Departmental layout
2. Flow of work
3. Work plan layout
4. Utilization of manpower
5. Work methods
6. Materials handling
7. Utilization of equipment
8. Motion economy

Corrective Techniques
1. Study with scale model
2. Flow chart study
3. Motion analysis
4. Comparison of units produced to standard allowance
5. Methods analysis
6. Flow chart and equipment study
7. Down time vs. running time
8. Motion analysis

M. A Planning Checklist
1. Objectives
2. Controls
3. Delegations
4. Communications
5. Resources
6. Manpower

7. Equipment
8. Supplies and materials
9. Utilization of time
10. Safety
11. Money
12. Work
13. Timing of improvements

N. Five Characteristics of Good Directions
In order to get results, directions must be:
1. Possible of accomplishment
2. Agreeable with worker interests
3. Related to mission
4. Planned and complete
5. Unmistakably clear

O. Types of Directions
1. Demands or direct orders
2. Requests
3. Suggestion or implication
4. volunteering

P. Controls
A typical listing of the overall areas in which the supervisor should establish controls might be:
1. Manpower
2. Materials
3. Quality of work
4. Quantity of work
5. Time
6. Space
7. Money
8. Methods

Q. Orienting the New Employee
1. Prepare for him
2. Welcome the new employee
3. Orientation for the job
4. Follow-up

R. Checklist for Orienting New Employees   Yes   No
1. Do you appreciate the feelings of new employees when they first report for work?   ___   ___
2. Are you aware of the fact that the new employee must make a big adjustment to his job?   ___   ___
3. Have you given him good reasons for liking the job and the organization?   ___   ___
4. Have you prepared for his first day on the job?   ___   ___
5. Did you welcome him cordially and make him feel needed?   ___   ___

		Yes	No
6.	Did you establish rapport with him so that he feels free to talk and discuss matters with you?	___	___
7.	Did you explain his job to him and his relationship to you?	___	___
8.	Does he know that his work will be evaluated periodically on a basis that is fair and objective?	___	___
9.	Did you introduce him to his fellow workers in such a way that they are likely to accept him?	___	___
10.	Does he know what employee benefits he will receive?	___	___
11.	Does he understand the importance of being on the job and what to do if he must leave his duty station?	___	___
12.	Has he been impressed with the importance of accident prevention and safe practice?	___	___
13.	Does he generally know his way around the department?	___	___
14.	Is he under the guidance of a sponsor who will teach the right way of doing things?	___	___
15.	Do you plan to follow-up so that he will continue to adjust successfully to his job?	___	___

S. Principles of Learning
  1. Motivation
  2. Demonstration or explanation
  3. Practice

T. Causes of Poor Performance
  1. Improper training for job
  2. Wrong tools
  3. Inadequate directions
  4. Lack of supervisory follow-up
  5. Poor communications
  6. Lack of standards of performance
  7. Wrong work habits
  8. Low morale
  9. Other

U. Four Major Steps in On-The-Job Instruction
  1. Prepare the worker
  2. Present the operation
  3. Tryout performance
  4. Follow-up

V. Employees Want Five Things
  1. Security
  2. Opportunity
  3. Recognition
  4. Inclusion
  5. Expression

W. Some Don'ts in Regard to Praise
1. Don't praise a person for something he hasn't done.
2. Don't praise a person unless you can be sincere.
3. Don't be sparing in praise just because your superior withholds it from you.
4. Don't let too much time elapse between good performance and recognition of it

X. How to Gain Your Workers' Confidence
Methods of developing confidence include such things as:
1. Knowing the interests, habits, hobbies of employees
2. Admitting your own inadequacies
3. Sharing and telling of confidence in others
4. Supporting people when they are in trouble
5. Delegating matters that can be well handled
6. Being frank and straightforward about problems and working conditions
7. Encouraging others to bring their problems to you
8. Taking action on problems which impede worker progress

Y. Sources of Employee Problems
On-the-job causes might be such things as:
1. A feeling that favoritism is exercised in assignments
2. Assignment of overtime
3. An undue amount of supervision
4. Changing methods or systems
5. Stealing of ideas or trade secrets
6. Lack of interest in job
7. Threat of reduction in force
8. Ignorance or lack of communications
9. Poor equipment
10. Lack of knowing how supervisor feels toward employee
11. Shift assignments

Off-the-job problems might have to do with:
1. Health
2. Finances
3. Housing
4. Family

Z. The Supervisor's Key to Discipline
There are several key points about discipline which the supervisor should keep in mind:
1. Job discipline is one of the disciplines of life and is directed by the supervisor.
2. It is more important to correct an employee fault than to fix blame for it.
3. Employee performance is affected by problems both on the job and off.
4. Sudden or abrupt changes in behavior can be indications of important employee problems.
5. Problems should be dealt with as soon as possible after they are identified.
6. The attitude of the supervisor may have more to do with solving problems than the techniques of problem solving.
7. Correction of employee behavior should be resorted to only after the supervisor is sure that training or counseling will not be helpful.

8. Be sure to document your disciplinary actions.
9. Make sure that you are disciplining on the basis of facts rather than personal feelings.
10. Take each disciplinary step in order, being careful not to make snap judgments, or decisions based on impatience.

AA. Five Important Processes of Management
1. Planning
2. Organizing
3. Scheduling
4. Controlling
5. Motivating

BB. When the Supervisor Fails to Plan
1. Supervisor creates impression of not knowing his job
2. May lead to excessive overtime
3. Job runs itself—supervisor lacks control
4. Deadlines and appointments missed
5. Parts of the work go undone
6. Work interrupted by emergencies
7. Sets a bad example
8. Uneven workload creates peaks and valleys
9. Too much time on minor details at expense of more important tasks

CC. Fourteen General Principles of Management
1. Division of work
2. Authority and responsibility
3. Discipline
4. Unity of command
5. Unity of direction
6. Subordination of individual interest to general interest
7. Remuneration of personnel
8. Centralization
9. Scalar chain
10. Order
11. Equity
12. Stability of tenure of personnel
13. Initiative
14. Esprit de corps

DD. Change

Bringing about change is perhaps attempted more often, and yet less well understood, than anything else the supervisor does. How do people generally react to change? (People tend to resist change that is imposed upon them by other individuals or circumstances.

Change is characteristic of every situation. It is a part of every real endeavor where the efforts of people are concerned.

1. Why do people resist change?
   People may resist change because of:
   a. Fear of the unknown
   b. Implied criticism
   c. Unpleasant experiences in the past
   d. Fear of loss of status
   e. Threat to the ego
   f. Fear of loss of economic stability

2. How can we best overcome the resistance to change?
   In initiating change, take these steps:
   a. Get ready to sell
   b. Identify sources of help
   c. Anticipate objections
   d. Sell benefits
   e. Listen in depth
   f. Follow up

II. Brief Topical Summaries

   A. Who/What is the Supervisor?
      1. The supervisor is often called the "highest level employee and the lowest level manager."
      2. A supervisor is a member of both management and the work group. He acts as a bridge between the two.
      3. Most problems in supervision are in the area of human relations, or people problems.
      4. Employees expect: Respect, opportunity to learn and to advance, and a sense of belonging, and so forth.
      5. Supervisors are responsible for directing people and organizing work. Planning is of paramount importance.
      6. A position description is a set of duties and responsibilities inherent to a given position.
      7. It is important to keep the position description up-to-date and to provide each employee with his own copy.

   B. The Sociology of Work
      1. People are alike in many ways; however, each individual is unique.
      2. The supervisor is challenged in getting to know employee differences. Acquiring skills in evaluating individuals is an asset.
      3. Maintaining meaningful working relationships in the organization is of great importance.
      4. The supervisor has an obligation to help individuals to develop to their fullest potential.
      5. Job rotation on a planned basis helps to build versatility and to maintain interest and enthusiasm in work groups.
      6. Cross training (job rotation) provides backup skills.

7. The supervisor can help reduce tension by maintaining a sense of humor, providing guidance to employees, and by making reasonable and timely decisions. Employees respond favorably to working under reasonably predictable circumstances.
8. Change is characteristic of all managerial behavior. The supervisor must adjust to changes in procedures, new methods, technological changes, and to a number of new and sometimes challenging situations.
9. To overcome the natural tendency for people to resist change, the supervisor should become more skillful in initiating change.

C. Principles and Practices of Supervision
1. Employees should be required to answer to only one superior.
2. A supervisor can effectively direct only a limited number of employees, depending upon the complexity, variety, and proximity of the jobs involved.
3. The organizational chart presents the organization in graphic form. It reflects lines of authority and responsibility as well as interrelationships of units within the organization.
4. Distribution of work can be improved through an analysis using the "Work Distribution Chart."
5. The "Work Distribution Chart" reflects the division of work within a unit in understandable form.
6. When related tasks are given to an employee, he has a better chance of increasing his skills through training.
7. The individual who is given the responsibility for tasks must also be given the appropriate authority to insure adequate results.
8. The supervisor should delegate repetitive, routine work. Preparation of recurring reports, maintaining leave and attendance records are some examples.
9. Good discipline is essential to good task performance. Discipline is reflected in the actions of employees on the job in the absence of supervision.
10. Disciplinary action may have to be taken when the positive aspects of discipline have failed. Reprimand, warning, and suspension are examples of disciplinary action.
11. If a situation calls for a reprimand, be sure it is deserved and remember it is to be done in private.

D. Dynamic Leadership
1. A style is a personal method or manner of exerting influence.
2. Authoritarian leaders often see themselves as the source of power and authority.
3. The democratic leader often perceives the group as the source of authority and power.
4. Supervisors tend to do better when using the pattern of leadership that is most natural for them.
5. Social scientists suggest that the effective supervisor use the leadership style that best fits the problem or circumstances involved.
6. All four styles—telling, selling, consulting, joining—have their place. Using one does not preclude using the other at another time.

7. The theory X point of view assumes that the average person dislikes work, will avoid it whenever possible, and must be coerced to achieve organizational objectives.
8. The theory Y point of view assumes that the average person considers work to be a natural as play, and, when the individual is committed, he requires little supervision or direction to accomplish desired objectives.
9. The leader's basic assumptions concerning human behavior and human nature affect his actions, decisions, and other managerial practices.
10. Dissatisfaction among employees is often present, but difficult to isolate. The supervisor should seek to weaken dissatisfaction by keeping promises, being sincere and considerate, keeping employees informed, and so forth.
11. Constructive suggestions should be encouraged during the natural progress of the work.

E. Processes for Solving Problems
1. People find their daily tasks more meaningful and satisfying when they can improve them.
2. The causes of problems, or the key factors, are often hidden in the background. Ability to solve problems often involves the ability to isolate them from their backgrounds. There is some substance to the cliché that some persons "can't see the forest for the trees."
3. New procedures are often developed from old ones. Problems should be broken down into manageable parts. New ideas can be adapted from old one.
4. People think differently in problem-solving situations. Using a logical, patterned approach is often useful. One approach found to be useful includes these steps:
   a. Define the problem
   b. Establish objectives
   c. Get the facts
   d. Weigh and decide
   e. Take action
   f. Evaluate action

F. Training for Results
1. Participants respond best when they feel training is important to them.
2. The supervisor has responsibility for the training and development of those who report to him.
3. When training is delegated to others, great care must be exercised to insure the trainer has knowledge, aptitude, and interest for his work as a trainer.
4. Training (learning) of some type goes on continually. The most successful supervisor makes certain the learning contributes in a productive manner to operational goals.
5. New employees are particularly susceptible to training. Older employees facing new job situations require specific training, as well as having need for development and growth opportunities.
6. Training needs require continuous monitoring.
7. The training officer of an agency is a professional with a responsibility to assist supervisors in solving training problems.

8. Many of the self-development steps important to the supervisor's own growth are equally important to the development of peers and subordinates. Knowledge of these is important when the supervisor consults with others on development and growth opportunities.

G. Health, Safety, and Accident Prevention
1. Management-minded supervisors take appropriate measures to assist employees in maintaining health and in assuring safe practices in the work environment.
2. Effective safety training and practices help to avoid injury and accidents.
3. Safety should be a management goal. All infractions of safety which are observed should be corrected without exception.
4. Employees' safety attitude, training and instruction, provision of safe tools and equipment, supervision, and leadership are considered highly important factors which contribute to safety and which can be influenced directly by supervisors.
5. When accidents do occur, they should be investigated promptly for very important reasons, including the fact that information which is gained can be used to prevent accidents in the future.

H. Equal Employment Opportunity
1. The supervisor should endeavor to treat all employees fairly, without regard to religion, race, sex, or national origin.
2. Groups tend to reflect the attitude of the leader. Prejudice can be detected even in very subtle form. Supervisors must strive to create a feeling of mutual respect and confidence in every employee.
3. Complete utilization of all human resources is a national goal. Equitable consideration should be accorded women in the work force, minority-group members, the physically and mentally handicapped, and the older employee. The important question is: "Who can do the job?"
4. Training opportunities, recognition for performance, overtime assignments, promotional opportunities, and all other personnel actions are to be handled on an equitable basis.

I. Improving Communications
1. Communications is achieving understanding between the sender and the receiver of a message. It also means sharing information—the creation of understanding.
2. Communication is basic to all human activity. Words are means of conveying meanings; however, real meanings are in people.
3. There are very practical differences in the effectiveness of one-way, impersonal, and two-way communications. Words spoken face-to-face are better understood. Telephone conversations are effective, but lack the rapport of person-to-person exchanges. The whole person communicates.
4. Cooperation and communication in an organization go hand in hand. When there is a mutual respect between people, spelling out rules and procedures for communicating is unnecessary.
5. There are several barriers to effective communications. These include failure to listen with respect and understanding, lack of skill in feedback, and misinterpreting the meanings of words used by the speaker. It is also common

practice to listen to what we want to hear, and tune out things we do not want to hear.
6. Communication is management's chief problem. The supervisor should accept the challenge to communicate more effectively and to improve interagency and intra-agency communications.
7. The supervisor may often plan for and conduct meetings. The planning phase is critical and may determine the success or the failure of a meeting.
8. Speaking before groups usually requires extra effort. Stage fright may never disappear completely, but it can be controlled.

J. Self-Development
1. Every employee is responsible for his own self-development.
2. Toastmaster and toastmistress clubs offer opportunities to improve skills in oral communications.
3. Planning for one's own self-development is of vital importance. Supervisors know their own strengths and limitations better than anyone else.
4. Many opportunities are open to aid the supervisor in his developmental efforts, including job assignments; training opportunities, both governmental and non-governmental—to include universities and professional conferences and seminars.
5. Programmed instruction offers a means of studying at one's own rate.
6. Where difficulties may arise from a supervisor's being away from his work for training, he may participate in televised home study or correspondence courses to meet his self-development needs.

K. Teaching and Training
1. The Teaching Process
Teaching is encouraging and guiding the learning activities of students toward established goals. In most cases this process consists of five steps: preparation, presentation, summarization, evaluation, and application.

   a. Preparation
   Preparation is two-fold in nature; that of the supervisor and the employee. Preparation by the supervisor is absolutely essential to success. He must know what, when, where, how, and whom he will teach. Some of the factors that should be considered are:
   1) The objectives
   2) The materials needed
   3) The methods to be used
   4) Employee participation
   5) Employee interest
   6) Training aids
   7) Evaluation
   8) Summarization

   Employee preparation consists in preparing the employee to receive the material. Probably the most important single factor in the preparation of the employee is arousing and maintaining his interest. He must know the objectives of the training, why he is there, how the material can be used, and its importance to him.

b. Presentation
   In presentation, have a carefully designed plan and follow it. The plan should be accurate and complete, yet flexible enough to meet situations as they arise. The method of presentation will be determined by the particular situation and objectives.

c. Summary
   A summary should be made at the end of every training unit and program. In addition, there may be internal summaries depending on the nature of the material being taught. The important thing is that the trainee must always be able to understand how each part of the new material relates to the whole.

d. Application
   The supervisor must arrange work so the employee will be given a chance to apply new knowledge or skills while the material is still clear in his mind and interest is high. The trainee does not really know whether he has learned the material until he has been given a chance to apply it. If the material is not applied, it loses most of its value.

e. Evaluation
   The purpose of all training is to promote learning. To determine whether the training has been a success or failure, the supervisor must evaluate this learning.
   In the broadest sense, evaluation includes all the devices, methods, skills, and techniques used by the supervisor to keep himself and the employees informed as to their progress toward the objectives they are pursuing. The extent to which the employee has mastered the knowledge, skills, and abilities, or changed his attitudes, as determined by the program objectives, is the extent to which instruction has succeeded or failed.
   Evaluation should not be confined to the end of the lesson, day, or program but should be used continuously. We shall note later the way this relates to the rest of the teaching process.

2. Teaching Methods
   A teaching method is a pattern of identifiable student and instructor activity used in presenting training material.
   All supervisors are faced with the problem of deciding which method should be used at a given time.

   a. Lecture
      The lecture is direct oral presentation of material by the supervisor. The present trend is to place less emphasis on the trainer's activity and more on that of the trainee.

   b. Discussion
      Teaching by discussion or conference involves using questions and other techniques to arouse interest and focus attention upon certain areas, and by doing so creating a learning situation. This can be one of the most

valuable methods because it gives the employees an opportunity to express their ideas and pool their knowledge.

c. Demonstration
The demonstration is used to teach how something works or how to do something. It can be used to show a principle or what the results of a series of actions will be. A well-staged demonstration is particularly effective because it shows proper methods of performance in a realistic manner.

d. Performance
Performance is one of the most fundamental of all learning techniques or teaching methods. The trainee may be able to tell how a specific operation should be performed but he cannot be sure he knows how to perform the operation until he has done so.
As with all methods, there are certain advantages and disadvantages to each method.

e. Which Method to Use
Moreover, there are other methods and techniques of teaching. It is difficult to use any method without other methods entering into it. In any learning situation, a combination of methods is usually more effective than any one method alone.

Finally, evaluation must be integrated into the other aspects of the teaching-learning process.

It must be used in the motivation of the trainees; it must be used to assist in developing understanding during the training; and it must be related to employee application of the results of training.

This is distinctly the role of the supervisor.

www.ingramcontent.com/pod-product-compliance
Lightning Source LLC
Chambersburg PA
CBHW080323020526
44117CB00035B/2632